PRIVATE FILES OF THE STARS

PRIVATE FILES OF THE STARS

JOHN SACHS
Piers Morgan

An Imprint of HarperCollins*Publishers*

For my daughters
Kimberley Georgina Sachs and Charlotte Adelaide Sachs

ACKNOWLEDGEMENTS

*Thank you to all those who were so helpful in putting this
ambitious project together especially Jacquie Quafe and all
the team at Ferret 'n' Spanner, Gary Farrow, Bernard
Docherty, Carlton at BKO, Ollie Smallman & Nick
Flemming, Dave Hogan, Billy MacLeod — London Records,
Geoff Baker — MPL, Siobhan Bailey, Raymond Edwards of
Marshall Arts, Julie Glover at Queen Productions, Bobby
Coppin, Amanda Pete and the team at CBS, Chris Mason
and all the team at WEA Records, Myra and team at MCA,
James and team at Phonogram and Adam and team at
Virgin.*

AN ANGUS & ROBERTSON BOOK
First published in the United Kingdom by
Angus & Robertson (UK) in 1991
An imprint of HarperCollinsPublishers Ltd
First published in Australia by
Collins/Angus & Robertson Australia in 1991
A division of HarperCollinsPublishers
(Australia) Pty Ltd

Angus & Robertson (UK)
16 Golden Square, London, W1R 4BN
United Kingdom
Collins/Angus & Robertson Publishers Australia
Unit 4, Eden Park, 31 Waterloo Road,
North Ryde, NSW 2113, Australia
William Collins Publishers Ltd
31 View Road, Glenfield, Auckland 10,
New Zealand

British Library Cataloguing in publication Data
Sachs, John
  Private files of the stars.
  1. Pop music – Biographies – Collections
  I. Title II. Morgan, Piers
  782.421640922

ISBN 0 207 16941 1

Printed in the UK by
Scotprint Ltd, Musselburgh
Typeset in the UK by New Faces, Bedford

CONTENTS

FOREWORD BY
LISA STANSFIELD

When John and Piers first approached me to take part in this book, I wasn't too sure about some of the more intimate questions! But it was great fun reminding myself of some of the amazing things that have happened to me. I never thought I would let anyone see my school report, let alone reveal the horrors of my first kiss! But they persuaded me, and they have persuaded some of the biggest names in the pop world to reveal their secrets too. It's a great idea for a book.

It's impossible to believe that this spotty unshaven teenager became one of the biggest stars rock has ever seen — George Michael

The signs were there, George Michael points upwards while his ex-Wham! pal Andrew Ridgeley heads downwards

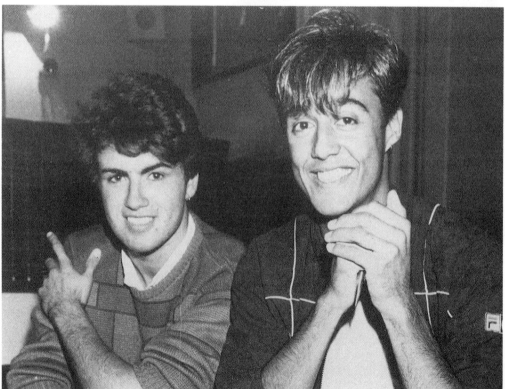

George Michael

REAL NAME: Giorgios Kyriakou Panayiotou.

BORN: 25/6/1963. Cancer. Finchley, North London.

HEIGHT: 5ft 11ins.

NICKNAME: My friends call me 'Yog', and Andrew Ridgeley calls me 'TLTI' which stands for The Legend That Is. It's a mickey-take because I got so much attention during the Wham! days.

SCHOOL: I was good when I was young, but gradually deteriorated as I got older. I was pathetic by the time I left! But I scraped through the exams I needed. I fell madly in love with my schoolteacher, Mrs Wilson, when I was about six years old. She was lovely but I don't think she felt quite the same way about me.

FIRST JOBS: I had loads of jobs. I was a cinema usher, a DJ in a restaurant, and even a labourer on a building site. I left that after two days because I hated it. I also had a Saturday job at British Home Stores but got the sack for not wearing a shirt and tie in the stock room, believe it or not. It was so depressing — I was middle class and it was the first time I realized that people from 'Coronation Street' did exist. I also worked as barman at my father's restaurant in Edgware but was sacked for giving wrong drink measures.

INTO THE BIZ: I formed a band called the Executive with Andrew Ridgeley and a few other schoolmates.

FIRST PERFORMANCE: Our very first show was at the Bushey Meads School scout hut on bonfire night, 1979. We played a lot of ska stuff and it seemed to go down pretty well.

MOST NERVE-WRACKING EXPERIENCE: Being driven by Andrew Ridgeley, and getting drunk with him in Los Angeles in 1987. I was a bit depressed so we went out and I got so drunk I was sick. I collapsed but woke up feeling fine!

GREATEST MOMENT: Wham!'s farewell concert at Wembley in London in June 1986. And the time I went carol-singing round London pubs with thirty mates wearing an assortment of wigs. I had a hippie one, like Neil from 'The Young Ones' except with a beard. We sang mainly Beatles' songs, very badly and got a terrible reception. A bus conductor tried to throw us off the bus — he had a fit. But it was brilliant fun, a lot of people knew it was me but couldn't believe it! I looked such an idiot.

BIGGEST COCK-UP: I was banned from Ascot racecourse when I turned up with dad without a tie. They eventually let me in, but asked me to watch from the back of the stand. The irony was that I was wearing a £300 suit!

CAR: Mercedes sports and a Range Rover. I can't remember the first one.

HOME: North London and Santa Barbara, California

HOLIDAYS: Anywhere hot. I like going back to Greece, and the South of France.

FOOD: Sweet and sour pork balls, Mars bars and mayonnaise.

DRINK: Herbal tea to soothe my voice.

MUSIC: Elton John and Paul McCartney.

FIRST RECORD: 'The Right Thing to Do' by Carly Simon in 1973. I bought it in a record shop when we were on holiday in Cyprus.

FAVE RECORDS: 'The Young Americans' by David Bowie, and 'Love Machine' by the Miracles.

FILM: *ET* was really excellent.

HOBBIES: Dancing, clubbing and drinking.

ADMIRES: Elton John — he was the first pop star I ever saw in concert. It was at Earls' Court in 1976 and he was brilliant then and he is brilliant now.

AMBITION: I'd like to be one of the best known artists of my time. I always wanted to be a pilot, but I'm partially colour blind.

HATES: 'Bad Boys' — one of Wham!'s first singles. I hated that record, it's like an albatross around my neck. 'Bad Boys' and the *Fantastic* album were the worst points in my career. I couldn't see the wood for the trees. I didn't know what I was doing.

FANCIES: That would be telling.

WILDEST PARTY: Wham!'s farewell concert party at the Hippodrome — it was unbelievable.

FIRST KISS: When I was eleven, I went out with a girl called Lesley Bywaters who was in my class at school. I looked a lot older than eleven and we used to go up to clubs in London, like the Global Village and Cherries. But we only went out for about two months. The first time I kissed her I don't think I enjoyed it particularly. I was too shocked.

FIRST SEXUAL EXPERIENCE: I lost my virginity at thirteen. I remember thinking, what is all the fuss about? I was overweight with puppy fat and thick glasses — and hopeless with women. She was a right old dog. I was so young and inexperienced that it was embarrassingly bad.

MADONNA

FULL NAME: Madonna Louise Ciccone.

BORN: 16/8/1958. Leo. Bay City, Michigan.

HEIGHT: 5ft 4ins.

NICKNAME: Father called me 'Nonny'.

SCHOOL: I used to have to go to church before going to Rochester Adams High School every day and my dad didn't let me watch TV until I was in my teens. I learned the piano and I was a cheerleader for the school team but I couldn't bear that.

FIRST JOBS: I worked at Burger King and McDonald's and was a lifeguard and scooped ice cream. I was sacked for squirting jam over a customer. I was so poor I used to scavenge in the dustbins after work for burgers we had thrown out. And I was once a painter's model. I took all my clothes off and they pretended to draw my body artistically. I posed for nude photos too, and got paid £10 an hour whereas I got £1.50 at Burger King.

INTO THE BIZ: I went to New York to dance school with just £30 on me, a giant baby doll and a photo of my mother who died when I was very young.

FIRST PERFORMANCE: Lead roles in *My Fair Lady* and *Sound of Music* at Rochester Adams High School.

MOST NERVE-WRACKING EXPERIENCE: When my loft caught fire in New York. I was sleeping on the floor surrounded by electric heaters when I woke up to find the carpet on fire. I jumped up and threw water everywhere — then my nightgown caught fire. I had to whip off all my clothes to save myself.

GREATEST MOMENT: Going to a Bowie concert, my first show, at Cobo Hall in Detroit. It was the most marvellous thing I'd ever seen in my life though I was punished severely for going.

BIGGEST COCK-UP: When my left breast popped out during a concert in Madrid. There were a lot of British football fans in the audience and they started chanting: 'Get your tits out for the lads'. I was really embarrassed.

CARS: My first was a battered old Chevrolet worth about £10. Now I drive a Mercedes sports for fun.

HOMES: First was in Detroit, now I live in a beachside home in Malibu and an apartment in New York.

HOLIDAYS: I love California.

Who's that girl? Raunchy Madonna cuddles up to gender-bender Marilyn at a New York party

FOOD: A chocolate sundae with lots of chocolate chip, hot fudge topping, whipped cream and nuts.

DRINKS: Carrot juice and the odd glass of champagne.

MUSIC: Vivaldi, Bach, Handel and Ella Fitzgerald. Also Diana Ross.

FIRST RECORD: 'The Letter' by Box Tops.

FAVE RECORD: 'Honky Tonk Woman' by the Stones. I used to give the boys at school lessons in how to be raunchy with that one.

FILM: *Brief Encounter.*

HOBBIES: Reading, jogging, swimming and dancing.

ADMIRES: Diana Ross.

AMBITION: I'd love to be a memorable figure in the history of entertainment in a sexual-comic-tragic way. I'd like to leave the impression that Marilyn Monroe did, to be able to arouse so many different feelings in people.

HATES: Polite conversation. And people who smoke in elevators. It is so rude.

FANCIES: Jon Bon Jovi, he is a hunk.

MOST FRIGHTENING MOMENT: When a madman with a gun was found in a crowd in New York minutes before I went on stage. He claimed he was a messenger from God. Luckily, the security men got him before he did anything. You are always aware that these sort of nutters might be out there but you have to ignore it.

WILDEST PARTY: The party to celebrate my movie *Shanghai Surprise.*

FIRST KISS: The first boy I ever loved was Ronny Howard in the fifth grade class. He had real white blond hair and sky blue eyes. He was so beautiful. I wrote his name all over my sneakers and on the playground. I used to take off the top part of my uniform and chase him around.

FIRST SEXUAL EXPERIENCE: My first real boyfriend was a graffiti artist called Norris Burroughs in New York when I was seventeen. He was wonderful.

Michael Jackson

FULL NAME: Michael Joseph Jackson.

BORN: 29/8/1958. Virgo. Gary, Indiana.

HEIGHT: 5ft 9ins.

NICKNAME: It's 'Smelly'. I was given that by Quincy Jones — but not because I smell. It's because I have a good nose for business.

SCHOOL: I really enjoyed school. My first ever singing performance was a version of 'Climb Every Mountain' at kindergarten — I was about four! The teachers were amazed by my voice — some of them were crying. I was so crazy about my teachers that I used to steal my mom's jewellery to give to them.

FIRST JOB: I was performing at five.

INTO THE BIZ: As you can imagine, my family was fairly musical! My earliest memory is having family sing-songs when the TV broke.

FIRST PERFORMANCE: My first professional performance was doing the Pass-The-Hat gigs with the Jackson Five.

MOST NERVE-WRACKING EXPERIENCE: I was messing around on the beach when I was young and I suddenly found myself unable to breathe. There was no air and I started to panic. I ran home and Jermaine took me straight to hospital. They found a blood vessel had burst in my lung. It was a condition related to pleurisy. Luckily, it has never recurred.

GREATEST MOMENT: Watching James Brown performing in concert. He was quite simply fantastic. He left me awe-struck, I knew every grunt, every spin, and every turn. Also, when Fred Astaire watched the video for 'Billy Jean' and rang me to say: 'Man, you are a hell of a mover. I used to do the same with my cane.' He invited me to his house and we watched his old movies. He was my hero.

MOST EMBARRASSING MOMENT: I was watching a strip show at the Apollo Theatre in New York. This girl had gorgeous eye lashes and long hair and she was putting on a great performance. Then at the end of it, she took off her wig, pulled a pair of big oranges out of her bra — and revealed a hard-faced guy under all the make-up. I was blown away!

CAR: I can't drive but I do own a Rolls Royce which Tatum O'Neal persuaded me to buy a few years ago.

HOME: I live in Encino, California.

HOLIDAYS: My favourite place is Disneyworld in Florida. I often go there in disguise and I have a permanent suite at the Park Royal Hotel nearby for when I stay over.

FOOD: I am a vegan, which means no meat, fish or eggs. I really like popcorn.

DRINK: I like orange juice but I don't like Pepsi, though I did the adverts for them.

MUSIC: I like virtually anything — from *Oklahoma* to Queen. I love Diana Ross and Stevie Wonder. My influences range from the Beatles to the Carpenters.

FIRST RECORD: 'Mickey's Monkey' by Smokey Robinson and the Miracles.

FAVE RECORDS: 'Yesterday' by the Beatles, Julie Andrews singing 'My Favourite Things' and Gordon McRae belting out 'Oh! What a Beautiful Morning'.

FILM: *ET* — the first time I saw it I cried my eyes out. All Spielberg films are great. I also loved *Oliver!*

HOBBIES: Working for the Jehovah's Witnesses and song-writing. I also collect pets. I've got a chimp called Bubbles, a llama called Louie, two deer, two dogs, a cat, a ram and four parrots.

ADMIRES: I wanted to meet Walt Disney but he died. And I wanted to meet Charlie Chaplin but he died too. There's nobody left that I would really want to meet. I've got no living heroes, but my friends include Elizabeth Taylor, Diana Ross, Jane Fonda, Brooke Shields and Tatum O'Neal.

AMBITION: To make a great film.

Michael Jackson has taught the world to dance — but here Jacko looks thriller-ed with his honorary degree

HATES: Smoking, drugs, alcohol. I have never tried any of them — if I want a kick I read a book or write a song.

MOST FRIGHTENING MOMENT: I set fire to my hair filming a Pepsi commercial in January 1984 when a special—effects bomb exploded on me. I was hospitalised while I had treatment for third-degree burns on my head. A fireman told me later than I could easily have died. Three months later I had some laser surgery at the Brotman Burn Centre to repair the damage to my head. They showed the advert anyway and President Reagan sent me a telegram saying how sorry he was to hear about the injury.

FIRST KISS: That's a secret!

SPANDAU BALLET

GARY KEMP

FULL NAME: Gary James Kemp
BORN: 16/10/1959. Libra. North London.
HEIGHT: 6ft.
NICKNAME: 'Gal'.
SCHOOL: I was good at English and got my maths O–level a year early. I won the music prize which annoyed all the other kids! But in the sixth form I was so devoted to the band I gave up academic studies.
FIRST JOBS: I was a paperboy at eleven, ran a greengrocer's with Martin for four years and I worked for the *Financial Times* as a prices clerk. I had to work out the dollar price against the pound and I got it wrong — it appeared in the paper wrong and caused absolute chaos! I was reprimanded but carried on.
INTO THE BIZ: I started off by stealing a snare drum from school — we used it on the first album, four or five years later. The first song I wrote was called 'Jesus Rode Through Nazareth'. I performed it in front of the then Bishop of Stepney, Trevor Huddleston!
MOST NERVE-WRACKING EXPERIENCE: Live Aid. We were all so hyped up — it was like losing your virginity. We had been looking forward to it so much, then it flashed past and we were left in a dazed sweat.
GREATEST MOMENT: Climbing Mont Blanc in 1987. It was purely an ego thing but getting to the top was a massive thrill. I climb as a hobby and do a lot of mountain walking.
BIGGEST COCK-UP: It was at a gig in Portugal. Our stage clothes didn't arrive so we ripped up sheets from the hotel in Lisbon and wore those. It was the New Romantic age so we got away with it. But it was very embarrassing on stage — God knows what they were wearing the next week in Portugal. Bedsheet headbands, probably.
CARS: An XR3 Ford Escort was the first, now I drive a Range Rover which is the best car I have ever sat in. It's so comfortable.
HOME: I live in Kentish Town in London in a Georgian house built in 1760.
HOLIDAYS: I like Thailand and Bali, where a mate of mine lives. I don't like

The Kray-ze Bunch. Spandau Brothers
Martin and Gary Kemp celebrate after
the première of their hit movie *The Krays*
with wives Shirlie and Sadie

beaches, I prefer a bit of culture in the mountains. I do love Rome and all that history.

FOOD: I am a vegetarian, a lacto. I eat dairy produce, beans, Thai, and Italian pasta. Our house is like *Gone With The Wind!*

DRINKS: Red wine. I used to drink too much Jack Daniels but now I stick to French and Spanish wine. And I am partial to Charles Heidsieck Champagne.

MUSIC: Classical to hip-hop. But I'm not into rock and roll or jazz, or dance. My favourite singer is Joni Mitchell.

FAVE RECORD: *Quadrophenia.*

FILM: *A Street Car Named Desire.*

HOBBIES: Climbing, keeping fit, reading, films.

ADMIRES: Steven Berkoff.

AMBITION: To have a happy family background and be a decent father.

HATES: People who don't go unleaded with their petrol.

FANCIES: Joanne Whalley-Kilmer, according to my wife Sadie! She knows who I ogle.

MOST FRIGHTENING MOMENT: I was caught in a mini-rock avalanche in the Atlas mountains in Morocco, which was very scary. And I remember all the police from my local station rushing round when I thought I was being burgled. They found a pigeon in a nest. I was too scared to look myself.

WILDEST PARTY: Toyah Wilcox's Mayhem Party in a warehouse in 1980. It was our second-ever gig and we were playing on the floor. I had condensation on my head and a skinhead staring me in the face for the whole gig — *very* unnerving. I also remember a lot of parties on the beaches of Bournemouth in the early eighties which were pretty wild.

FIRST KISS: I was five, with a girl called Julia. I locked her in the phone box at school because she wouldn't kiss me back. She was repulsed and that made me angry. My first proper girlfriend was a twelve-year-old called Debbie in my class. We went to the Planetarium together where it was nice and dark!

FIRST SEXUAL EXPERIENCE: I was seventeen, and it was almost as worrying as Live Aid. It was in a hotel room in Benidorm and it was not a very good experience. I didn't use a condom — it was all over too quickly. It was a drunken affair and no, I can't remember her name!

MARTIN KEMP

FULL NAME: Martin John Kemp.

BORN: 10/10/1961. Libra. In my mum's room in Islington, North London.

HEIGHT: 6ft.

NICKNAME: I don't have one.

SCHOOL: They were always saying I was very lethargic and could do better. I was good at artistic things and tech drawing, geography and maths, but I preferred sport. I played football for the First XI which meant I got away with doing less homework because all the teachers were soccer-mad.

FIRST JOBS: Gary and I appeared on *Jackanory* when I was eight and he was ten. On Saturdays we used to run a greengrocery together and I did a few newspaper rounds.

INTO THE BIZ: I was at Anna Scher's drama school for eight years. I wanted to be a professional footballer but Gary persuaded me to join his group. I couldn't play guitar but I learned the bass in four weeks.

FIRST PERFORMANCE: It was a strange experience. Amazingly I was very confident. It was at somebody's party at university. I was sixteen. We were called Gentry and it was the original Spandau line-up. We changed the name because Robert Elms told us to.

MOST NERVE-WRACKING EXPERIENCE: My first day at drama school when I was eight years old. Mum held my hand and led me in. It was terrible, I buried my face into mum's left buttock. I was so shy then.

GREATEST MOMENT: Watching the birth of my daughter. It was a natural birth. That was something you cannot compare with anything else. I wasn't doing any work the whole time Shirlie was pregnant so we went through the whole thing together. An incredible experience.

BIGGEST COCK-UP: I was doing a TV series with Tom Conti when I was fourteen called 'Glittering Prizes'. I was doing a shower scene and I was supposed to pee on the kid next to me. But I just couldn't go — it was impossible. It went on all day. Eventually a woman used a funnel to pour orange juice down my front. That was the last thing I did before *The Krays* — it put me off films!

CARS: A Lancia spider was the first. Now I have a Range Rover for my dog, a dobermann called after Emma Peel in 'The Avengers'.

HOMES: The first was in Islington. Now I live in my own North London place.

HOLIDAYS: My favourite would have to be the South of France. I love having croissants for breakfast and driving to Italy for pasta for lunch.

FOOD: Any sort of pasta — I don't eat meat, fish or chicken. I love Orso's in Covent Garden, London, a lovely place.

DRINK: Red wine, especially Nuit St. George.

MUSIC: Everything, really. I like different things for different moments. I love George Michael's voice, he could sing a bad song brilliantly.

FIRST RECORD: 'Me and my Life' by the Tremeloes. Terrible record, and when we had *The Krays* premiere, they were the band and they dedicated it to me! I was really embarrassed.

FAVE RECORD: 'Loving You' by Minnie Ripperton.

FILMS: *Raging Bull* with Robert De Niro, and all the Bond films.

HOBBIES: Playing guitar.

AMBITION: I had three ambitions as a kid — to be a pop star, an actor and to play football at Wembley. I finally achieved the last one when I played in a charity game there recently. I also want to play James Bond in a movie, the best role in Britain.

HATES: Being a Libran, I hate cruelty to animals. (I love my dog.)

FANCIES: Phoebe Cates, star of 'Lace'.

MOST FRIGHTENING MOMENT: Every time I get on an aeroplane. I hate the idea of flying. I can't stand the thought of things that heavy staying up in the air, but I just have to live with it. In six months, I caught 150 planes on the last tour. I kept thinking it must be this one . . .

WILDEST PARTY: John Keeble's stag night and wedding reception at Fred's Club. Me and my brother and my dad were all so drunk we couldn't walk.

FIRST KISS: In the playground at Brotherfield Junior School. I was a big fan of Kiss Chase behind the bike sheds. I was a late starter and didn't have much interest in girls. I had my first girlfriend when I was thirteen — I wrote in my diary that it was true love. It wasn't.

FIRST SEXUAL EXPERIENCE: It was terrible. I was seventeen. I will keep it private, though.

New Kids on the Block

New Kids on the Block, the hottest band
in the world, face the cameras at their first
British press conference

JOEY McINTYRE

FULL NAME: Joseph Mulrey McIntyre.
BORN: 31/12/1972. Capricorn. Needham, Massachusetts.
HEIGHT: 5ft 6ins.
NICKNAME: 'Joe Bird', 'Joey Joe', because Donnie thought I looked like a bird.
SCHOOL: I always got very good grades but I was always misbehaving in class.
By the end, I was doing a gig with the New Kids until four a.m., sleeping for two

hours and going to school. I never told them I was in a band. I had a big row with mum by the time tenth grade came — I refused to go to school because we had just had our first Top Ten hit in America. Now I have a tutor. I was always impersonating my principal teacher — one day she caught me and I got a whacking. I cried and pleaded for mercy but she wasn't having any of it.

FIRST JOBS: I used to rake leaves and I was a grocery boy.

INTO THE BIZ: I sang a song from *Oliver!* at the local children's theatre with my sister Carol. Mum was in the audience and cried when she heard us.

FIRST PERFORMANCE: At a prison on Deer Island, Massachusetts.

MOST NERVE-WRACKING EXPERIENCE: Breaking my ankle playing football — it was agony and I really thought I'd damaged it beyond repair. I could see my whole career going down the pan. Fortunately, it wasn't too serious.

GREATEST MOMENT: I bought mum a fur coat after we got our first seven-figure pay cheque. I went on holiday to Hawaii soon after that and she rang me up and said, 'Joseph, I'm walking around in your coat.' She loved it.

BIGGEST COCK-UP: Being asked for my autograph in the toilet. I couldn't believe it — this girl just walked in and said, 'Joey I love you, please sign this paper for me.' I replied that my hands were full!

New Kids real life block — number 1. Pint-sized Joey McIntyre lives in the smarter west side of Boston

CARS: I've got a Jaguar and a BMW with a portable phone.

HOME: Boston.

HOLIDAYS: The ultimate place to go has to be Disneyland. I love taking a girl I really like there and going on all the rides — you can't fail to have a good time and impress the girls!

FOOD: Mexican.

DRINKS: Coke, anything non-alcoholic.

MUSIC: Huey Lewis and the News, the Temptations.

FIRST RECORD: The Temptations album.

FAVE RECORD: 'The Power or Love' by Huey Lewis and the News.

FILMS: *Big, Beverley Hills Cop, Midnight Express.*

HOBBIES: Basketball and tenpin bowling.

ADMIRES: Robert De Niro, Bill Cosby, and my manager Maurice Starr.

AMBITION: I always wanted to be a bricklayer like my brother. Maybe I will be one day?

HATES: War and homelessness.

FANCIES: Michelle Pfeiffer, Jamie Lee Curtis and Jodie Whatley.

MOST FRIGHTENING MOMENT: Me and my mates used to play Mookalaka — which meant throwing sticky buds from plants at passing cars — the winner was the one who got most buds to stick. I never played it again after one driver stopped his car, chased after me and beat me up.

FIRST KISS: I went out with this girl for six months — I cried when it ended. I was twelve and she was eleven. Her name was Chrissie and we met in the children's theatre in Boston. But she decided to end it because I was spending too much time with my friends and not enough time with her.

FIRST SEXUAL EXPERIENCE: Not saying.

DONNIE WAHLBERG

FULL NAME: Donald E. Wahlberg.

BORN: 17/8/1969. Leo. Boston, Massachusetts.

HEIGHT: 5ft 10ins.

NICKNAME: 'Cheese'.

SCHOOL: I cheated for four years at Boston's William Trotter School. It was fun to cheat and I was good at it! I preferred sport to be honest. I remember having some teeth knocked out playing hockey — that hurt!

New Kids real life block — number 2. Donnie Wahlberg's family home in Boston, Mass.

FIRST JOBS: I had two. I worked in a bank doing foreign transactions, usually with England. And then for a shoe shop where I got an award for being absent. I was quite proud of that at the time.

INTO THE BIZ: I formed a band called Risk with two mates, Billy and Eric. We thought we were great, but we weren't. We played everything by ear, which didn't work out very well usually. I got an audition for the New Kids mainly because I could do brilliant Michael Jackson impressions.

FIRST PERFORMANCE: The first New Kids show was at a prison on Deer Island, Massachusetts. It was very unnerving but they loved us.

MOST NERVE-WRACKING EXPERIENCE: I was on a ride in an amusement park — the Ferris wheel. I was with a friend and it suddenly stopped at the top. We stayed there for ages and it was terrifying — everyone was screaming. But we got down in the end. I thought we'd had it at one stage, it was swaying all over the place. Ferris wheels are the most dangerous things in the world — I will never go on another one.

GREATEST MOMENT: Getting a standing ovation at New York's Apollo Theatre. It was a very important show for us and when the crowd went wild I felt a great thrill inside me.

BIGGEST COCK-UP: I remember seeing this girl in a wheelchair at the front of the stage and I eventually reached down to touch her. With that she leaped up and grabbed me — she had used the chair to get near me. Can you believe that? I felt conned.

CAR: A Saab 90.

HOME: Dorchester, Massachusetts.

HOLIDAYS: I love going home — that's a nice enough holiday.

FOOD: My dad's home cooking.

DRINKS: Water, apple juice, Coca-Cola. I get sick on alcohol.

MUSIC: I love all dance music and Bobby Brown and Janet Jackson.

FIRST RECORD: 'Space Cowboy' by Jonzon Crew.

FAVE RECORD: Anything by Janet Jackson.

FILM: *Scarface* with my favourite actor Al Pacino.

HOBBIES: Writing, drawing, baseball and basketball.

AMBITION: I always wanted to be a baseball player, perhaps I'll do that if the New Kids ever break up.

ADMIRES: My brother Jimmy who has now rehabilitated after being jailed for drugs. He committed various robberies and stuff under the influence of drugs and he was put in prison for a few years. Now he is back out and I am so proud of him. His success in quitting drugs is greater than anything I have ever done. I also admire my mum who has spent all her life trying to make her nine kids happy and she's done a great job of it.

HATES: Drugs. Three of my brothers have been in prison for drug-related offences and that has shown me how bad it can be. I was exposed to drugs when I was younger and on the streets but I said no because I had seen people's lives ruined.

FANCIES: Caron Wheeler, the ex-Soul II Soul singer. I danced with her at last year's *Smash Hits* party. And I really dig Cher, as well. But my favourite has to be Janet Jackson. I caught her in a hotel bathtub when we stayed in the same hotel recently — the other guys bet me to sneak into her room pretending to be a waiter. She went mad, then she realised it was me and laughed.

MOST FRIGHTENING MOMENT: In England on tour last year I went to a club and the owner picked up my Walkman and was messing around with it. I told him to put it down so he threw it at me and we started cursing each other. Then four BMWs full of dudes in suits pulled up outside and chased me out of the club. I didn't hide but I didn't want to get killed either.

FIRST KISS: My first girlfriend was called Wanda Pumpernickel and I met her at school in Boston. I was fifteen, she was fourteen and we loved each other. But then she left me for another guy. I cried for ages at the time — but I bet she's crying now!

FIRST SEXUAL EXPERIENCE: I'm not telling you that, man! She may hear about it and sell her story. But I'm a very sexual person. I've got a special pair of silk boxer shorts I always wear when I've met a nice girl and want to do the 'nasties'.

JORDAN KNIGHT

FULL NAME: Jordan Nathaniel Marcel Knight (mum took the first two names from the Bible).

BORN: 17/5/1970. Taurus. Worcester, Massachusetts.

HEIGHT: 5ft 10ins.

NICKNAME: 'J'.

SCHOOL: I liked maths and I used to read a lot. Art was my favourite subject but I wasn't a very good student. I used to be a graffiti vandal, always spraying walls and stuff. But I would be really clever and spray 'Jordan' on the wall. Dead giveaway, wasn't it? I was always in trouble, stealing candy bars with my mates and fighting. Luckily I never got caught.

FIRST JOB: I worked in an insurance company stuffing envelopes with rubbishy leaflets. It was terrible — so boring. I quit after about six months to work full time on the band.

INTO THE BIZ: I was really into acting at school and my first starring role was Charlie in *Charlie and the Chocolate Factory* at a local theatre. I loved being in and watching plays.

FIRST PERFORMANCE: At a prison on Deer Island, Massachusetts.

MOST NEVER-WRACKING EXPERIENCE: I was standing outside this store when I was about ten and these kids were writing on the wall. Suddenly the store owner ran out with a gun. He took one look at me and thought I had done it — then he pointed the gun at me and said he was going to shoot. I was so scared I ran straight home without stopping.

GREATEST MOMENT: Hearing a New Kids song on the radio for the first time and buying my mum a Lincoln Continental with the plate '4 U MA'. The look on her face was amazing.

BIGGEST COCK-UP: I remember being asked to sing my first solo for the school choir and the other kids suddenly realising how high my voice was. I was so embarrassed I never did it again. Now it's my trademark. Also, I once tripped and fell into the crowd during a show. The girls went wild and just tore me to pieces. It was terrible — I couldn't escape, it was very embarrassing.

CAR: A black Porsche 911.

HOME: First home was in a Boston suburb called Westwood. Me and three of my brothers shared a double bunk bed. I shared mine with Jon which was cool.

HOLIDAYS: Hawaii.

FOOD: Lasagna and tomato ketchup and chewing gum.

DRINKS: I like coke and milkshakes.

MUSIC: Malcolm McLaren, Prince, One Nation. And I used to love the Beatles' music, even though they were oldies by the time I got into them.

FIRST RECORD: 'Rapper's Delight'.

FAVE RECORD: 'You Make Me Feel Brand New' by the Stylistics.

FILMS: *Soul Man* and *Robocop.*

HOBBIES: Swimming, basketball.

ADMIRES: Robert De Niro — all his films are brilliant.

AMBITION: To be successful and to look after my family.

HATES: Prejudice and people who say I'm gay. They see my earrings, hear my voice and assume I am gay. But it's definitely not true. People say don't worry about it but I do — I don't want people thinking I'm a wimp.

FANCIES: Janet Jackson is lovely with a nice butt. I have met her a few times and she's a real cutie.

MOST FRIGHTENING MOMENT: My mum used to be a social worker dealing with some of the toughest kids in our district. One of them pulled a knife on her one day and she called for help. I rushed in and just attacked him — dragging the knife out of his hand. I didn't have time to be scared until afterwards, but he wasn't a bad kid really — he had obviously been doing drugs and didn't know what he was doing. We lived in a rough area — mum and my sister were both mugged at knifepoint right outside our house.

Guess who? Jordan (back row, third from left) and Jon Knight (front row, left) posing with their family when they were very new kids

FIRST KISS: Her name was Pam and we met at a summer camp where I was working helping young kids. I was thirteen, she was fourteen, and we went steady for four months until she ditched me for someone else at summer camp. She taught me to kiss, how to move our tongues around. It was peachy and has proved useful lately.

FIRST SEXUAL EXPERIENCE: No way am I telling you that.

JON KNIGHT

FULL NAME: Jonathan Rashleigh Knight.

BORN: 29/11/1968. Sagittarius. Worcester, Massachusetts.

HEIGHT: 5ft 11ins.

NICKNAME: 'Jizz' or 'Rinse'.

SCHOOL: I won a prize for writing a poem about Santa Claus but I was quite a naughty pupil — in the ninth grade I threw dead squids, frogs and starfish down the heating vent and the whole school stank for weeks. I liked science but I didn't get very good grades.

FIRST JOBS: I used to be a cleaner in Burger King. I got the job because my sisters worked there, but I was only twelve so most of the jobs I did were illegal. Then I got a job in a restaurant helping the chef. I ended up being head chef, cooking everything from spaghetti to hamburgers. I worked four or five days a week and the tips were brilliant.

INTO THE BIZ: A guy called Herb, who was the director of a summer camp near us, taught me a lot about music, especially how to sing.

FIRST PERFORMANCE: At a prison on Deer Island, Massachusetts. I had severe stage fright and didn't eat for a week before that show. My knees were knocking so loudly when I went on stage that I was worried the microphone would pick it up.

MOST NERVE-WRACKING EXPERIENCE: When I was fifteen my parents divorced and that was a really difficult time for me. I left school because of it and went to pieces a bit. I think they wanted to get divorced all along but dad felt a responsibility to us kids so he didn't leave until we had grown up a bit.

GREATEST MOMENT: Buying my grandfather, Floyd Putnam, a new house in Florida. He refused to take it saying I didn't owe him anything — but I told him I had already bought it so he had no choice in the matter. There were tears in his eyes when I gave him the keys and that made me feel real good.

New Kids real life block — number 3. Jon and Jordan Knight's sumptuous mansion in Dorchester, Boston

BIGGEST COCK-UP: I was sitting in a Jacuzzi in a big hotel and suddenly all these girls spotted me and stood there watching me. I couldn't get out — it was like being in an aquarium. I felt like a fish, it was so embarrassing. And I remember another time I was trying to impress this girl and took a pouch of cash when we went on a date. Unfortunately, the pouch split and all the money spilled everywhere.

CAR: A black BMW 735. I had a car crash with Jordan when I was sixteen. He was driving and it hurt my back so bad I still have problems with it when I am dancing.

HOME: I live with mum in Dorchester, Massachusetts.

HOLIDAY: Hawaii.

FOOD: Burger King, chocolate cake and Italian food.

DRINK: Milkshakes — chocolate and strawberry.

MUSIC: R and B, Tiffany, Janet Jackson.

FIRST RECORD: 'Mickey Mouse Sings'.

FAVE RECORD: 'My Prerogative' by Bobby Brown.

FILM: *Jumping Jack Flash* and *Soul Man*.

HOBBIES: Swimming, skiing and basketball.

AMBITION: To carry on with what we are doing.

ADMIRES: Tiffany. Meeting her for the first time when we supported her on tour was great. We were really nervous because we wanted to make a good impression. She was really sweet, though, and we got along great. And I really admire Maurice Starr, our manager, who is a genius.

HATES: Eggs, war.

FANCIES: Janet Jackson, Farah Fawcett, Tina Turner — she's old but she's got class — Madonna and Tiffany.

MOST FRIGHTENING MOMENT: When a thousand screaming girls caught me and Jordan outside an arena and tried to rip all our clothes off — that was terrifying.

FIRST KISS: A small, petite black girl who I used to walk to school. Her name was Dolores and I would kick the ball down her end of the street just to catch a glimpse.

FIRST SEXUAL EXPERIENCE: My first real girlfriend was Thea Richardson. I fought with Donnie over her and won.

DANNY WOOD

FULL NAME: Daniel William Wood.

BORN: 14/5/1969. Taurus. Boston, Massachusetts.

HEIGHT: 5ft 7ins.

NICKNAMES: 'Puff McCloud', 'Woody the Woodpecker' or 'Zitto' because of my spots.

SCHOOL: I remember my English teacher Mr Millman, who was brilliant. He hated textbooks and most of the lessons would be verbal. I got a four-year scholarship to Boston University which I can go back to later if I want. I got awards for best maths student, and I was captain of the school soccer team. But my favourite school

New Kids real life block — number 4. Danny Wood's discreet pad on the northern side of Boston

memory is punching the school bully in the mouth and knocking his teeth out. He had been provoking me for months. I was a bit of a tearaway when I was younger. I even got busted for stealing clothes but I was let off jail because I was underage. That was when I learned my lesson.

FIRST JOBS: I used to work in summer camp teaching six-year-old kids how to breakdance. I also worked in a pizza place, making them. And I was a courier selling airline tickets for a while — but I quit when 'Please Don't Go, Girl' became a hit.

INTO THE BIZ: I sang John Lennon's 'Imagine' at our graduation ceremony — very scary. Then I joined a school band called Rock Against Racism with all sorts of kids — black, Hispanic, etc.

FIRST PERFORMANCE: At a prison on Deer Island, Massachusetts. It was petrifying, especially as many of the prisoners thought we were a joke to start with.

MOST NERVE-WRACKING EXPERIENCE: I was fourteen and on a bike trip. We were climbing over these old army camps when I slipped. It was 50ft down and I hung on to a rock by my fingertips. Thankfully help was close by.

GREATEST MOMENT: Buying my parents a twelve-day holiday in Hawaii, my sister gold jewellery and my brother a car last Christmas.

BIGGEST COCK-UP: Falling on a teddy bear during the British tour and breaking my foot — that was so-o-o-o-o stupid. It hurt a lot too — but that was more my pride than anything else.

CAR: A Cherokee Jeep.

HOME: My first home was a three-decker in Boston, Massachusetts. I bought it off my dad a year ago.

HOLIDAY: Hawaii.

FOOD: Roast beef, Chinese, pork rinds and salt and vinegar crisps. Junk food.

DRINK: Water is the only thing I ever drink.

MUSIC: One Nation, David Bowie.

FIRST RECORD: 'Let's Dance' by David Bowie.

FAVE RECORD: Sister Sledge's first album.

FILMS: *Terminator*, *Star Wars* and *Trading Places*.

HOBBIES: Breakdancing — I used to be the only white kid breakdancing in my neighbourhood.

ADMIRES: Kevin Costner, Cher.

AMBITION: I always wanted to be an architect when I was younger. Now I would like to be a top recording engineer.

HATES: Prejudice and stealing and drugs. I used to be offered drugs all the time on the street but I refused so often the other kids used to call me 'Do-Good Wood'.

FANCIES: Leila K. and Paula Abdul.

MOST FRIGHTENING MOMENT: I get scared stupid by horror films — especially *The Shining*. I was with this girl in the cinema and I was more terrified than she was. I don't know why I keep going to horror movies — but I suppose I must like being scared.

FIRST KISS: Her name was Beth Gadet and I was six years old. She had a soup bowl haircut, that's all I remember.

FIRST SEXUAL EXPERIENCE: Not saying — she might come after me.

GLORIA ESTEFAN

FULL NAME: Gloria Maria Estefan.

BORN: 1/9/1957. Virgo. Havana, Cuba. My family lost everything in the revolution so we left for Miami when I was very young.

HEIGHT: 5ft 4ins.

NICKNAMES: The band call me 'Major Burns' after the character in 'M*A*S*H'. It's because I'm such a perfectionist.

SCHOOL: I went to a convent school and it was run by a really obnoxious nun. She weighed 600 pounds and had a moustache. She was real mean and I was terrified of her. If I ever saw her walking towards me I used to run a mile. I still bear the emotional scars from that woman. My favourite subject was reading — I loved Shakespeare and Emily Brontë. I had no confidence when I was younger — I was plump, wore glasses and couldn't talk to boys.

FIRST JOBS: I once trained to be a psychologist. I couldn't handle it because I immediately associated myself with the cases. I saw a lot of people with problems that I couldn't do anything about, and it really depressed me. I don't think I was cut out for it. I also worked as a Spanish and French interpreter for the customs department in an American airport. My most difficult customer was an Italian nun who I found trying to smuggle a large sausage under her habit. The poor woman didn't speak any English and was scared that she wouldn't like American food.

INTO THE BIZ: I have always been musical — it seemed natural to go into the business.

Tina Turner shows why she is rock's most glamorous granny with another sizzling stage show

Meet my new backing singer — Basil Fawlty! Tina Turner larks about with John Cleese, her favourite funny-man

Gary Kemp out on the town with his stunning wife Sadie

Martin Kemp shows a bit of the Spandau Ballet style with wife Shirlie

New Kids Donnie Wahlberg and Joe McIntyre
show they are hangin' tough

Freddie Mercury stars with his biggest hero —
opera singer Montserrat Caballé

Mick Fleetwood and Samantha Fox at the ill-
fated BRIT awards — it was a disaster

*The Lady and The Tramp . . . scruff Bob Geldof
with his beautiful wife Paula Yates*

The biggest superstar of them all — Michael Jackson

Annie Lennox in the South of France — she's still
one of the classiest ladies in rock

Oh Mona! Heart-throb Craig McLachlan strums his guitar on another hit record

Lady in red — stunning Gloria Estefan shows the style that has made her one of the world's most successful female artists

FIRST PERFORMANCE: It was in Miami — it went very well, if I remember, though I was incredibly nervous.

MOST NERVE-WRACKING EXPERIENCE: I almost drowned while scuba diving around a wrecked ship in Florida. I got tangled up in the cables and old rigging inside the ship and couldn't break loose. I could feel the air running out as I struggled to get free — I was frightened I would die underwater. Luckily some friends noticed I hadn't come back up and sent down a search party to rescue me. I still love diving but that incident is always on my mind — I have recurring nightmares about it.

GREATEST MOMENT: My first concert appearance.

BIGGEST COCK-UP: I once went topless on live TV. I flashed my breasts on nation-wide Mexican telly. We were performing this song and my bando top just slipped down and I didn't realize until I put my hand there. Someone from the side of the stage nipped across and gave me a safety pin to pin my top up. It was so embarrassing. I don't wear bando tops any more.

CARS: We have three — a Mercedes, a Brazilian sports car, and a 1980 Rolls Royce Silver Shadow.

HOMES: My first home was in Cuba. Now I live on Star Island in Miami, Florida. My husband Emilio and I took four years to build it from scratch.

HOLIDAYS: I love it where I am. My idea of a holiday is sitting at home doing nothing.

FOOD: I love to cook and I'm not bad at it. I love Cuban food like rice, beans, and refried beans. I'm not supposed to eat that because I put on weight. But I treat myself once a month.

DRINK: I don't drink very much but I like good wine.

MUSIC: Prince, Diana Ross.

FIRST RECORD: It was probably a Spanish album of some sort.

FAVE RECORD: Dionne Warwick's 'Walk On By'.

FILM: I liked *Batman* — Jack Nicholson's great.

HOBBIES: I love diving and going off in my boat down to the Bahamas.

ADMIRES: My husband Emilio — he is my best friend.

AMBITION: I would like to do a movie. I've had lots of offers but I am very wary of them. I have no idea how to act!

HATES: I can never understand why people in the front five rows of concerts have binoculars. It's like what can you be looking at that close?

FANCIES: My husband Emilio — he's gorgeous.

MOST FRIGHTENING MOMENT: When I lay on the floor of my tour bus last year and realized I had broken my back. I'm also terrified of heights. I had to do a video while standing on top of a skyscraper once and it scared the life out of me.

FIRST KISS: I don't know why, but I wasn't popular with boys at school. I was a bit of an ugly duckling. My first boyfriend was called Juan Carlos. He lived opposite us and all the girls on the street fancied him. I was about twelve at the time. My mum didn't tell me anything about the birds and bees. Whenever I asked my mum where babies come from she'd always chicken out and avoid telling me. One day she came home with a huge encyclopaedia called *The Life Cycle Library*. It was full of explicit little diagrams which explained everything.

FIRST SEXUAL EXPERIENCE: My husband Emilio is my one and only lover. I was a shy eighteen-year-old when I met him and he preferred older women. But we fell in love. The first time we made love I wasn't nervous or frightened — it just felt right. I think you know when you are in love with someone. Emilio brought me out of my shell.

Phil Collins

FULL NAME: Phillip David Charles Collins.

BORN: 30/1/1951. Aquarius. Chiswick, London.

HEIGHT: 5ft 8ins.

NICKNAME: 'Thumper'.

SCHOOL: I went to the Barbara Speake stage school in West London. My mum was a teacher there — and still is. I was a bit of a lad when I was young — me and my mates used to nick drink and cigarettes from the local off-licence by distracting the girl who worked there. I was about ten then but I soon grew out of it.

FIRST JOB: I've never really had a job — not a real job. My first professional job was playing the Artful Dodger.

INTO THE BIZ: My aunt Daisy used to give me piano lessons. But I really wanted to be a drummer so I sold my train set and bought a set of drums.

FIRST PERFORMANCE: Artful Dodger when I was eleven years old in the West End show *Oliver!* I had to pull out after eleven months when my voice broke. I told mum and dad that I wanted to be a drummer in a rock group which they assumed meant a life of sex, drugs and rock and roll. They were so upset, they didn't speak to me for two weeks! My first screen performance was as an extra in *A Hard Day's Night.* Paul McCartney doesn't believe me, but it's true.

MOST NERVE-WRACKING EXPERIENCE: Probably when my wife Jill went into labour six days early. The car stalled at a junction and wouldn't start again. So I ran a mile and a half to a garage to borrow a car and it was closed. Eventually I ran back to my car, kicked it very hard and it started! Jill did finally get to the hospital and everything went fine. It was more of a trauma for me than her, I think!

GREATEST MOMENT: Playing a half-hour set at Buckingham Palace for Prince Charles' fortieth birthday party. It was wall-to-wall royalty — I even saw the Queen jive to Bill Haley's 'Rock Around the Clock'. I was surprised but it was a magical moment and showed she could be like everyone else. She's a very good jiver — in fact Elton John told me he had jived with her himself. LIve Aid, too, was great. I was the only person to play at both shows, in London and Philadelphia, thanks to Concorde. It was a fantastic experience.

MOST EMBARRASSING MOMENT: I was a little uncomfortable about playing the nude scenes with Julie Walters in *Buster.* They wanted me to be naked but I wasn't having any of that so I insisted on wearing underpants with flesh-coloured tights on top. They were uncomfortable and crushed any passion that may have been in the air. And I find early footage of Genesis very embarrassing. It looks so awfully pretentious. But at the time a lot of people didn't think so.

CARS: The first was an old Morris Minor. Now I've got a seven-year-old BMW, a Nash Metropolitan that Robert Plant gave me and an A35 Austin which cost me £1,200. I like old cars.

HOMES: My first home was a three-bedroomed house in Hounslow, North London. Now I live in a Georgian farmhouse in Sussex.

HOLIDAYS: Going home is a holiday!

FOOD: I like Japanese sashimi — that's raw fish — a good curry, and lemon grass soup from Thailand.

DRINK: I like a nice whisky before I go to bed but not when I'm touring — it sticks in the throat when you get up in the morning.

MUSIC: I'm into most things — jazz, classical, pop, rock. But I've always loved the Beatles, I suppose.

FIRST RECORD: 'Please Please Me' by the Beatles.

FAVE RECORDS: The Beatles' Revolver album, that's the one I love the most. And the soundtrack to the film *Romeo and Juliet*.

FILMS: *Romeo and Juliet* and anything with Jack Nicholson, who's my favourite. Also *The Alamo* with John Wayne brings tears to my eyes.

HOBBIES: I don't have time for much. I tried fishing with Eric Clapton once but I haven't got the patience. Another mate, Nick Faldo, is always trying to get me on the golf course — but I suspect that is because he wants drumming lessons! I go to watch Spurs whenever I can. I've got a tennis court and like the odd game.

ADMIRES: My heroes were always the Beatles. I used to stand in front of my mirror pretending to be John Lennon. I also admire Michael Jackson and the Prince and Princess of Wales, of course.

AMBITION: Just to carry on with what I'm doing.

HATES: I hate seeing people who are high on drugs at my concerts. It makes my blood boil. It's particularly bad in Germany where you can smell the marijuana before you get on stage. Drugs are such a stupid waste of time.

FANCIES: I've always had a soft spot for Madonna. It's that mixture of a soft innocent voice and the sexy underwear. I met her once in Los Angeles but she seemed very nervous.

MOST FRIGHTENING MOMENT: Whenever I meet snakes — and I have this terrible fear of dying in an underground tube tunnel.

FIRST KISS: Her name was Lynda and I was eleven. She was my first love but

Phil Collins clowns around with his sister and brother Clive

One of Phil Collins' less 'popular' cars — this Ford Popular only lasted a couple of trips

sadly she didn't love me. I remember walking a long way from the station to her house and knocking on the door just to say, 'Hi, you don't want to go out with me do you?' She would say, 'No,' I'd say, 'Fine.' She'd close the door and I would walk home again! It ended in tears.

FIRST SEXUAL ENCOUNTER: Cheryl when I was fourteen — she was a girl from the Barbara Speake stage school.

TINA TURNER

REAL NAME: Anna Mae Bullock.

BORN: 26/11/1939. Sagittarius. Nut Bush, Tennessee.

HEIGHT: 5ft 4ins.

NICKNAME: 'The Duchess'.

SCHOOL: Primary school in Flagg Grove, Nut Bush. I left school very early because the family needed money.

FIRST JOBS: When I was still at school I used to clean houses at weekends. I worked as a maid for one family in Tennessee for a year.

INTO THE BIZ: When I met Ike Turner in St. Louis, aged eighteen.

FIRST PERFORMANCE: It was with Ike Turner's band in Memphis.

MOST NERVE-WRACKING EXPERIENCE: The first time I did a scene with Mel Gibson in *Mad Max* — it was terrifying, far worse than singing live. And I remember filming a video on Copacabana Beach in Brazil when this nut waded towards me in the water and shouted: 'I want to kiss you.' There were security men all over the water trying to reach this guy and me thinking: what the hell's going on here? But he was harmless as it turned out.

GREATEST MOMENT: Reaching number one with 'What's Love Got To Do With It'.

CARS: My first was a Ford Thunderbird, now I've got a Mercedes Jeep.

HOMES: First was a small apartment in East St. Louis, now I have a £600,000 house in Notting Hill, West London which I love. It's a five-storey Georgian place.

HOLIDAYS: I love Egypt with all the pharaohs and pyramids.

FOOD: Thai and Italian.

DRINKS: Champagne and coffee.

MUSIC: ZZ TOP, AC/DC, all heavy metal and I love Sam Cooke's voice.

FIRST RECORD: A B. B. King album.

FAVE RECORD: 'Dancing In The Dark' by Bruce Springsteen.

FILMS: *Casablanca, Blade Runner.*

HOBBIES: Interior decorating, especially on my own house.

ADMIRES: The Rolling Stones, Steve Winwood and Mark Knopfler. I also love Prince Charles. He once told me I had the best legs he had ever seen — I told him he wasn't so bad himself.

AMBITION: To be a ballerina.

HATES: Answering the phone, polyester clothing and hotel rooms.

MOST FRIGHTENING EXPERIENCE: When I found a lump in my breast two years ago. I was terrified about having the test and so relieved when they said I was OK. In the end, it was a bit like going to the dentist.

FIRST KISS: His name was Harry and he was a boy in the school basketball team. He wore the number nine shirt and I thought he was lovely. We went out for about a year then he dumped me for another girl, Theresa. He got her pregnant and said he had to marry her. When he told me I cried all day.

FIRST SEXUAL EXPERIENCE: I was fifteen and the boy was sixteen. It was in the back of a car in St. Louis. It hurt so much I could hardly move afterwards — but he wanted to make love three times. I couldn't believe it.

Mick Jagger, Tina Turner and David Bowie — three of the biggest stars in rock history

Freddie Mercury

REAL NAME: Frederick Bulsara

BORN: 5/9/1946. Virgo. Zanzibar, North Africa.

HEIGHT: 5ft 10ins.

NICKNAME: 'Freddie'.

SCHOOL: St. Peter's Boarding School, Bombay, India. I had excellent reports, of course! My favourite subjects were music, drama and sport. I later went to Ealing College of Art in London and got a diploma in graphics and illustration. I was table tennis champion at college.

FIRST JOB: Selling clothes in Kensington Market.

INTO THE BIZ: I got in through sheer talent!

FIRST PERFORMANCE: I joined a school band called the Hectics when I was fourteen.

MOST NERVE-WRACKING EXPERIENCE: Playing to 300,000 people in Rio — it was amazing! My worst moment was when I had to cancel a show in Sun City, South Africa after just fifteen minutes because my voice packed in. It was a sell-out crowd and I was in the middle of 'Under Pressure'. I felt terrible about it and cried afterwards at the thought of letting so many people down. It was almost as bad as the time when my leg went on stage in Germany. I had to be carried off stage and the others continued without me.

GREATEST MOMENT: Live Aid — it was a fantastic day and the atmosphere was excellent.

BIGGEST COCK-UP: The funniest was when customs men at Heathrow searched my bag and found nail polish, mascara, jewellery and black satin panties! It was my stage gear but they didn't believe it. I also remember when I met Prince Andrew at the Crush Bar in the Royal Opera House, Covent Garden, London. I was wearing a white scarf and I didn't realise it had actually gone into my drink. Prince Andrew eventually reached over, removed the scarf and wrung it dry. Then he laughed and said: 'I think that's better, Freddie!' He later asked me to sing but I said I would only do that if he swung from the chandelier. He didn't!

CAR: I can't drive! I have a chauffeur-driven Mercedes.

HOMES: Zanzibar was the first. Now I live in Kensington, West London. I bought it for £500,000 fifteen years ago and was offered £4 million for it by an Arab, the same year! Elton John told me to sell it, but I resisted. Now I can't imagine selling it.

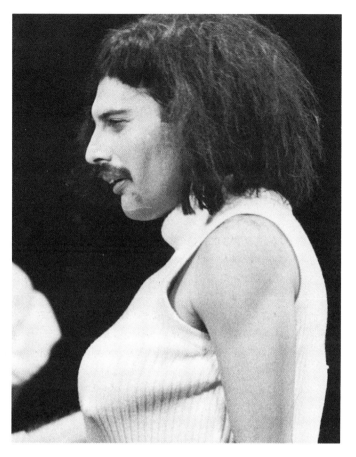

Outrageous Freddie Mercury dons a wig and Dolly Parton cleavage for one of his typically flamboyant Queen performances

HOLIDAY: Japan — it's a wonderful place.

FOOD: Spicy Indian and Japanese.

DRINKS: Vodka — and iced Stolychnaya.

MUSIC: I like Tears for Fears, and Aretha Franklin is the greatest singer ever. I also adore opera, especially Montserrat Caballé and Placido Domingo. I used to like Michael Jackson but we lost touch after I recorded some songs for his *Thriller* album and he never used them. I don't think he understood my sense of humour!

FAVE RECORDS: 'Natural Woman' by Aretha Franklin and 'Careless Whisper' by George Michael.

FILM: *Some Like it Hot.*

HOBBIES: Koi carp, Japanese art, antiques and cat collecting. I have six cats!

ADMIRES: Jimi Hendrix, John Lennon, Paganini and Beatrix Potter. I also admire Rod Stewart and Elton John. We were going to call ourselves Hair, Nose and Teeth

but couldn't agree over billing. Naturally I wanted it to be Teeth, Hair and Nose!
AMBITION: To be a boring old fart and to carry on as I am!
HATES: Sliced white bread and boring people.
FANCIES: Marilyn Monroe.
WILDEST PARTY: Usually my birthday parties, but there have been too many to remember the wildest.
MOST FRIGHTENING MOMENT: My first ride in a helicopter in 1982 was terrifying. I also remember when two girl fans pulled at my scarf at the same time after a New York show and virtually strangled me.
FIRST KISS: Not telling!
FIRST SEXUAL EXPERIENCE: Certainly not telling you that either!

BRIAN MAY

FULL NAME: Brian Harold May.
BORN: 19/7/1947. Cancer. Hampton, Middlesex.
HEIGHT: 6ft 2ins.
NICKNAME: My mates call me 'B'.
SCHOOL: I was good at physics and astronomy and I was talkative in class — reports always said I talked too much. I ended up with twelve O–levels and four A–levels. I also liked drama. I played women in the plays because it was an all-boys' school. I swam for the school but didn't like sport.
FIRST JOBS: I worked in a windscreen wiper factory off the Bath Road to earn cash in the holidays. I also worked for EMI in their ballistics department dabbling in defence.
INTO THE BIZ: I was playing with people from school in a group called Smile at London University. The tennis player Roger Taylor answered my call for a drummer on the school notice board. We played all the colleges. Then I met Freddie in 1969 and we formed Queen.
FIRST PERFORMANCE: At a lecture hall in Imperial College. It was supposed to be a showcase but no music biz people turned up. We played fairly heavy stuff like 'If I Were A Carpenter' and one we wrote called 'Aeroplane Noises In E'! It was Fred's idea to call us Queen. We didn't like it at the time but it served the function of being memorable.

MOST NERVE-WRACKING EXPERIENCE: There have been lots of frightening things in my life but getting separated from my wife and kids was pure hell. I haven't really got over it yet — that is an honest answer.

GREATEST MOMENT: Probably the Knebworth gig we did in 1987 during the last European tour. And the Rock in Rio gig in front of 300,000 people. It felt like something out of this world. It was like being taken to the moon. I can't really describe it.

BIGGEST COCK-UP: We played this gig up north when the night was split between us and a disco. We were asked not to go on for the second half because the kids preferred the disco. We got £20 that night.

CARS: My first was a Volvo P 1800E, red. It was hell to drive. Now I drive a Mercedes TE estate, it's the only thing I can get my kids Jimmy, Louisa and Emily into.

HOMES: The first was a semi-detached in Feltham, in Middlesex. Now I live out of town in Surrey which is very quiet. I have a few holiday homes.

HOLIDAYS: Disneyworld with the kids. That was great.

FOOD: I am more or less a vegetarian. I like Japanese and Chinese food too, chop suey and chow mein.

DRINK: Lager, Saporo and Guinness.

MUSIC: I like heavy rock, Hendrix and Cream, Van Halen and Def Leppard; and for singers, John Lennon, Tina Turner, Freddie Mercury and Joe Cocker.

FIRST RECORD: My dad bought me 'The Rock Island Line' by Lonnie Donegan.

FAVE RECORD: It would be the Beatles' *White Album*.

FILM: *Back To The Future I* and *Batman*.

HOBBIES: Collecting old photographs, stereo photos from the 1850s and the 1860s. I identified with those photographers as being the pop stars of their day.

ADMIRES: Sinead O'Connor's song 'Nothing Compares to You' really impressed me. It was completely masterly. I have listened to it over and over again and it's brilliant. It stunned me totally. And the singer from the Chimes is wonderful, too. There are a lot of very talented women out there at the moment.

AMBITION: Acting and writing. I would like to put my own passion into something like that.

HATES: Traffic and wasted time.

FANCIES: Natalie Wood was captivating in *Rebel without a Cause*.

MOST FRIGHTENING MOMENT: I remember my little girl Louisa falling down a mountain in the Alps after swinging on a metal fence outside a restaurant. One minute she was there, the next I heard this thump. Complete fear grabbed hold of

Former 'Eastenders' star Anita Dobson out on the town with long-time love Brian May — the Queen guitarist — and his son

me, but I found her safe about 12ft further down the mountain face, flat on her back in the snow. She hadn't even realised what had happened.

WILDEST PARTY: It was at the Queen's Hotel in New Orleans in 1978. We were celebrating conquering America and every strange act under the sun was flown in to be there. One guy's act was to hide in liver and pretend to be a piece of liver. And there were various girls doing various things with their bodies. I spent most of the night looking for a girl who hadn't turned up. Lots of bizarre people used to come to our parties — very weird and very enlightening. It opened my eyes to the whole thing. I was a young boy who had no idea. I remember a *bloke* propositioning me as I came off stage. I had never come into contact with gays. This very handsome guy said 'Will you sleep with me tonight?' I was completely dumbstruck! We used to meet loads of transvestites too.

FIRST KISS: I was fifteen or sixteen — a late developer and I had had a very sheltered upbringing. It was an awful experience. I was only doing it because I thought everyone else was doing it. Angela was her name. I found it so unappetising it put me off for about a week. But the next week when I went out with someone else it was a lot better. The Hollies were being played at a party at the time and whenever I hear that record I get those insecure feelings of being a young boy again. I used to feel very out of place at dances — I went on stage to avoid all that crap! The whole sexual arena was very intimidating. I became a guitarist because I couldn't dance. My first girlfriend was Pat, I was sixteen and went out with her for four years, amazingly enough.

FIRST SEXUAL EXPERIENCE: It was good because I loved the girl. The problem was that I didn't think I should be doing it. I never slept with Pat in the whole four years we were together. Part of me wanted to but I had been told it was wrong. I was at least twenty-one. After I left Pat I met a great girl, and I remember it happening at the college digs. I woke up feeling so depressed and horrified I couldn't live with myself — but I soon got used to the idea! I am still very close to the girl concerned so I won't name her.

Mick Fleetwood

FULL NAME: Michael John Kells Fleetwood
BORN: 24/6/42. Cancer. Redruth, Cornwall.
HEIGHT: 6ft 5ins.
NICKNAME: 'Micky'.
SCHOOL: I went to a public school called Sherborne. I was particularly good at fencing and acting. But I was always running away. Once, I walked for more than twenty miles through the Sussex Downs before the police caught me.
FIRST JOB: At Liberty's store in London. I worked on the sanctions desk answering phones from people who wanted to spend thousands of pounds. I lasted three weeks.
FIRST PERFORMANCE: In a band called the Senders at Notting Hill Gate youth club. We played Shadows stuff — all instrumental then. We were payed £6 a week and promised a free bowl of spaghetti.
MOST NERVE-WRACKING EXPERIENCE: At the Marquee with the early

Fleetwood Mac. I have trouble finding the beat of songs. I lost all sense of beat and I couldn't get back. It turned into a nightmare. In the end Peter Green put my hand into the right position on the guitar.

GREATEST MOMENT: Playing in front of 70,000 people at Wembley Stadium, I knew that would probably be the last time we would all play together on stage in Britain.

BIGGEST COCK-UP: Taking drugs. I spent a fortune on them and it was such a waste of time and money.

HOME: I live in Malibu, where I have been for the last ten years.

HOLIDAYS: I love New Mexico — there's a feeling of space and the scenery is the best in America.

CAR: I've got a Jeep.

FOOD: I eat almost anything.

DRINK: I used to be an alcoholic but I hardly touch the stuff any more. I feel a lot better for it, too.

MUSIC: I am a great fan of Marvin Gaye, George Harrison and John Lennon (in and out of the Beatles). I also like Keith Richards' solo album, and the Stones generally. I tend to go back to the older stuff.

FIRST RECORD: Elvis Presley, I think.

Mick Fleetwood looks more like the grim reaper than one of the world's top rock stars — at the BPI awards in 1988

FAVE RECORD: It would have to be something by the Beatles.

MOST FRIGHTENING EXPERIENCE: I was stalked by a madman in America. He was a very scary guy who followed me everywhere. I was terrified the whole time he was around me. He showed me one of our album covers once and said: 'See that photo? It might be your head but it's my torso.' That scared me.

FIRST SEXUAL EXPERIENCE: I was seventeen and I remember it very well. I was practically raped by this very attractive twenty-three-year-old called Susanne Boffey. She saw me at a gig and basically said 'I want you.' She took me back to her place in Chelsea and that was that. Amazingly, I saw her again ten years later when I was visiting John McVie in the Virgin Islands. She was in a disco. We had a chat and laughed about that first time. She still had the marble head I'd given her. A very interesting girl, just a raving sex maniac.

LISA STANSFIELD

FULL NAME: Lisa Jane Stansfield.

BORN: 11/4/1966. Aries. Manchester.

HEIGHT: 5ft 6ins.

NICKNAME: 'Peanut Head' — it's because I have a very small head. I don't mind it really . . .

SCHOOL: I went to Bullough More Primary School in Harewood and all the boys used to tease me about how small my boobs were — I used to stand in front of the mirror saying grow, grow. But they never did, unfortunately.

FIRST JOB: I was a barmaid at the Hare and Hounds in Rochdale but I got sacked on my first night because I was giving people more change than they were giving me. I was not a good economical asset!

INTO THE BIZ: My mum played Motown records all the time. One of my first performances was doing a summer season with Freddie Starr but it was so awful I quit after two weeks.

FIRST SHOW: At a private party at mum and dad's house. I was very nervous but I think it went pretty well.

MOST NERVE-WRACKING EXPERIENCE: Performing at the Radio City Music Hall in New York. I had to sing live at a party for my record company, Arista

Records, and Whitney Houston and Dionne Warwick were on the same bill. That was scary.

GREATEST MOMENT: A show I did in Newcastle last July — it was the best I have ever done.

BIGGEST COCK-UP: I fell over a little child presenting 'Razzmatazz' on ITV when I was fourteen. I was running around with all these kids and I went flying off-screen. I also remember stumbling across a nudist beach in France when I was very young. It was more embarrassing for mum really. I was swimming with my sister and we saw this guy with his willy out. I told mum and she went bright red!

CARS: My first car was a Fiat 127, now I am using a Cortina which belongs to my boyfriend's mum.

HOMES: My first home was an old police house in Harewood, now I live with Ian in Rochdale.

HOLIDAYS: I just like relaxing — it doesn't matter where.

FOOD: Spicy food is my favourite — especially Indian. I love a nice biryani with a hot curry sauce.

DRINK: Dry white wine, especially Frascati.

MUSIC: I love all soul music — my favourites are Chakka Khan, Aretha Franklin and Gladys Knight.

FIRST RECORD: Donny Osmond's 'Puppy Love'. I worshipped him when I was young.

FILM: *Brazil* with Jonathan Pryce.

HOBBIES: Watching movies and walking.

ADMIRES: Nelson Mandela — he is a remarkable man.

AMBITION: To make a film.

HATES: I hate people who don't do their job properly. I suffer fools badly, especially if they let me down.

FANCIES: Anthony Perkins from *Psycho* is very sexy, and Bob Hoskins.

MOST FRIGHTENING MOMENT: I was bullied at school by another girl. It was awful — she really gave me a terrible time until I pushed her down some steps at school and she never touched me again. Funnily enough, I saw her again a few years ago and you never forget, do you? I really wanted to whack her but I didn't.

WILDEST PARTY: We had an amazing fancy dress at our house, the theme was minor celebrities. I went as Anthea Redfern and we all got extremely drunk. It was a very funny night.

FIRST KISS: It was a boy called James Woodward and I nearly threw up when I kissed him and realised that tongues were involved. I was about twelve and we

Delighted Lisa Stansfield collects another award after a triumphant year of hits all around the world

Redbrook School's music teacher was positively prophetic about the thirteen-year-old Lisa Stansfield's future!

REDBROOK SCHOOL

Name Lisa Stansfield   Form A5

Subject Music   Year Ending July 1979

What a pity that we did not discover Lisa's musical talent until recently. She obviously has a very good ear and has achieved good results in aural tests. Good luck in the future, Lisa!

R M Aspinall
~~Form~~/Subject Teacher

clashed at my local disco. My first real boyfriend was David Johnson. He is married now and lives in Rochdale.

FIRST SEXUAL EXPERIENCE: I am not going to tell you.

Roland Gift

FULL NAME: Roland Lee Gift.

BORN: 28/5/1962. Gemini. At my family home in Birmingham.

HEIGHT: 6ft.

NICKNAME: I was known as 'Guinness' because I had blond hair.

SCHOOL: I liked art and drama but I didn't think school was the best way for me to work. I swam quite a lot and I remember my music teacher thumping me for

Roland Gift clutches a well-earned beer
after collecting another huge pay cheque
for his Fine Young Cannibals hits

calling her a silly cow. She wouldn't let us talk during lunch — it was like being a Trappist monk. I used to get whacked with a cheese board. I was a naughty young lad. When I was seven, me and my mates stole some miniature Batmans and Robins from Woolworth's. And one night in Hull we stole an ice cream van. I was always going to Clash shows and getting into rucks. I had blond hair with a streak in it — punk. Once someone caught my earring and ripped my ear lobe.

FIRST JOB: I was a builder's labourer at sixteen. And I worked in markets as well.

FIRST PERFORMANCE: I put on a controversial play at school called *The Son of Satan*. In one scene, we pretended to cut this possessed kid's heart out — I even bought a pig's heart to make it more realistic.

INTO THE BIZ: I got together in 1977 with some mates and formed a band called Blue Kitchen. We were a punk outfit with a sax player! Later we changed the band's name to the Acrylics.

MOST NERVE-WRACKING EXPERIENCE: Getting on planes. Every time I get on one I am terrified. And I was scared stiff when we played in LA to a celebrity audience two years ago.

GREATEST MOMENT: Going to number one in America for the first time was great.

BIGGEST COCK-UP: It came when I was in the Acrylics and we hadn't performed for a while. I came on at the start of the set looking really cool and stood at the mike stand. The mike stand dropped to the floor and I looked like a real prat so I went off and came back on again.

CAR: First and only is a green Saab — I still drive it now.

HOME: I've just sold my nine-bedroom home in Archway, North London. I don't really have a home at the moment.

HOLIDAYS: Australia and New Zealand.

FOOD: I like fish. I think you should kill animals yourself if you want to eat meat.

DRINK: I'm a bit of a lager lout — I love beers, bitter as well. I can take a lot of booze. In my younger days I was always getting drunk.

MUSIC: Burt Bacharach songs, Dionne Warwick and Otis Redding.

FIRST RECORD: *Tighten Up Vol. 2.*

FAVE RECORD: Otis Redding's *Greatest Hits.*

FILM: *My Life as a Dog,* a Swedish film with sub-titles.

HOBBIES: My job is my hobby, it's not really like work.

ADMIRES: Actor Mark Rylance, who did a brilliant Hamlet, Daniel Day Lewis and Meryl Streep.

AMBITION: Make more music, movies and plays.

HATES: Interviews, racism and bigotry.

FANCIES: The star of *Sex, Lies and Videotapes* — I can't remember her name.

MOST FRIGHTENING MOMENT: Going on the dive bombers in a fairground with my mates. It was absolutely terrifying. And I remember being scared when I almost got seduced by a woman in Hyde Park when I was ten. Luckily I escaped.

WILDEST PARTY: In Hull at an art college student party. I was a punk and we decorated this bloke's room by moving the fridge, and repainting the room. Then we jumped out of the first floor window and went to another party!

FIRST KISS: I was five, she was called Linda. She said, 'Do you love me?' I said, 'Yeah.' And we kissed! I played kiss-chase a lot. One girl even did a strip show in the street for us.

FIRST SEXUAL EXPERIENCE: I was fifteen and at a party. The theme of the party was soldiers of love. I met this girl called Petra who was thirty and German. It was a very nice experience. I had always fancied her and she didn't disappoint me.

KIM WILDE

REAL NAME: Kim Smith

BORN: 18/11/1960. Scorpio. Chiswick, West London.

HEIGHT: 5ft 6ins.

NICKNAME: My brother and Marti call me 'Coo' as in 'Kimmy-Coo'. But don't call me Kimberley!

SCHOOL: I left school in 1980 with seven O–levels and one A–level in art. I used to sign quite a few reports in place of mum because I didn't want her to see them — but in fact they were all quite good. I think I'm such a high achiever because my family set such high standards.

FIRST JOBS: I debudded carnations in a greenhouse during O–levels on Saturdays for extra cash. I used to cycle there. And I cleaned for my piano teacher and at Lister Hospital in Stevenage.

INTO THE BIZ: My dad, Marti, had to blow out three days of studio time to do some gigs. So he told my brother Ricky to take the time, and I joined in. Dad was my influence from the start. The first time I was interested in singing was when I heard Cilla Black singing 'Anyone who had a Heart' at the age of four.

Subject	Effort	Term Marks	Position	Assessment
ENGLISH				
Reading	B+	—	2nd.	Very Good
Spelling	B+	83	3rd.	Good
Writing	E	81	4th.	Good
Comprehension	C?	7?	2?=	Very Good
Composition	A-	83	1st.	Very Good
Grammar, etc.	A-	8?	2nd=	Good
Literature	—			
HISTORY	A-	86	1st.	Very Good
GEOGRAPHY	A	78	1st.	Very Good
RELIGIOUS KNOWLEDGE	B	69	4th.	Good
FRENCH	—			
LATIN	—			
ARITHMETIC				
Mental	A-	8?	3rd.	Very Good
Mechanical	B+	57	4th.	Good
Problems	B+	53	5th.	Good
ALGEBRA	—			
GEOMETRY	—			
SCIENCE or NATURE STUDY	B+	81	1st.	Very Good

Note for Parents

Effort: Letter on five point scale A, B, C, D or E.
Assessment: Scale: **Excellent Very Good Good** Fair Weak
is based on work done and progress made.

GAMES AND PHYSICAL DEVELOPMENT
Very Good. Kim participates with eagerness.

ART Kim is keen and enthusiastic. Good.

HANDWORK Very Good. Kim devotes much time and energy to artistic expression.

MUSIC Good. An attentive pupil. M.D.

Attendance (Number of half days in Term 121)

No. of half days absent 15   No. of times late 0

Social Behaviour (Report by Form Master/Mistress)
Kim seems very happy in the school environ-
ment. She mixes well with her classmates
and makes good use of her free time.

General Assessment

Very pleasing progress.

P.S. Seager.
Headmaster/Mistress

Next Term 19?? Spring
Begins: Wednesday Jan. ?. (Half day. No school lunch.) ?.
Half Term Holiday: Fri. Feb. ? (noon) To Tues. Feb. ?5 (inclusive)
Ends: Wed. Mar. 26th.

Class Position 3rd

Kim Wilde's always been a bright spark —
even in 1968 her teachers were raving
about her performance

FIRST PERFORMANCE: In Australia at thirteen with dad, mum Joyce, Ricky and me singing 'Country Roads' and 'I'm So Lonesome'. We all took different harmonies. I drank in the applause. My first TV role was in a telly ad for smokeless fuel — I was about ten, I think.

MOST NERVE-WRACKING EXPERIENCE: Supporting Michael Jackson on his *Bad* tour, especially on the first night in Italy where they had never heard of me. He was very caring and incredibly vulnerable. It was such a great opportunity for me but Michael kept a distance from all of us including his band!

GREATEST MOMENT: When I won the BPI award for Best Female Vocalist in 1983 in front of Michael Jackson and Paul McCartney. I even beat Annie Lennox. I was very proud and was speechless on stage. I was absolutely choked when Angela Rippon gave the award to me.

BIGGEST COCK-UP: I remember when mum, who was an agent, was let down on a booking at a Bedford nightspot. Mum said, 'Do you and a friend want to earn

£40 each?' We said yes, sure, but we had no dance routine. I was called Rita, she was Wendy. We were following a troupe of ace black dancers. It was so embarrassing. But it was the cheapest anyone got Kim Wilde for. There was also the time when my boob popped out of my dress when I was on stage doing the Michael Jackson tour! I didn't realise what had happened so I didn't have cause to be embarrassed.

CARS: A ruby red Beetle was the first. Now I drive a Mitsubishi Shogun.

HOME: My flat in London.

HOLIDAYS: My best ever was a camping holiday five years ago in the South of France with five girlfriends — it was wild.

FOOD: Most of it, in all guises. Italian best of all — spaghetti vongole.

DRINK: Evian water, champagne and good wine.

MUSIC: Steely Dan.

FIRST RECORD: An Elton John or Gary Glitter record. I was in Gary's fan club.

FAVE ARTIST: Janet Jackson.

FAVE BOOK: Anything by Todd Rundgren.

FILM: *Some Like it Hot.*

HOBBIES: Painting on my lap! I like doing portraits.

HATES: I don't hate many things.

FANCIES: Christopher Lambert is really gorgeous, and Jeff Bridges is fanciable too.

MOST FRIGHTENING MOMENT: I had someone follow me in my car once and we got into the country lanes. I was desperate not to let him get in front of me. I drove very fast to escape.

WILDEST PARTY: My twenty-first at Knebworth House. Dad played on stage and so did some of his mates including Mickey Most. I also remember a brilliant party that Elton John threw for his manager John Reid. There were lots of fireworks.

FIRST KISS: David Summry. He was a local boy. I was crazy about him and he kissed me in a disco when I was twelve. It was a very tight-lipped affair.

FIRST SEXUAL EXPERIENCE: I had probably better leave it because the person concerned is a great friend of mine and his wife wouldn't like it very much!

Now she's one of the most beautiful singers in pop and at sixteen she was already showing signs that she'd be a star

Bob Geldof

FULL NAME: Robert Frederick Zenon Geldof.

BIRTH: 5/10/1954. Libra. Dublin, Ireland.

HEIGHT: 6ft 2ins.

NICKNAME: 'Iggy'.

SCHOOL: My school days were dire. I enjoyed absolutely nothing. I was thoroughly miserable. Eventually I left school, ran out of the gates and shouted with relief.

FIRST JOBS: I was a kitchen porter in a hotel in Dublin. Then I went on to work in a pea-shelling factory in Peterborough. Neither careers held much interest for me, I hasten to add.

FIRST PERFORMANCE: My first band was called the Farm. The first Boomtown Rats gig was on Halloween in 1975 in a classroom at Bolton St College. It went down very well.

MOST NERVE-WRACKING EXPERIENCE: The first concert the Rats played at the Hammersmith Odeon in London. It was the biggest show we had ever played and we were terrified. There have also been a series of brushes with the police. I've been arrested for selling dodgy hot dogs in Shaftesbury Avenue, for giving out political leaflets and for possession of cannabis. I was also nicked for whacking a bloke outside a hotel in Sweden who turned out to be the manager of the hotel. I didn't get the room.

GREATEST MOMENT: Going to number one with 'Rat Trap' — it fulfilled a dream.

BIGGEST COCK-UP: I was acutely embarrassed to be asked for my autograph while I was on the loo. A hand slipped through the open window and a voice said: 'Sign this, Bob.' What could I say?

CARS: I paid £5 for a Volkswagen which I drove for several years. My current car is a Saab turbo — it's done 90,000 miles and is completely knackered.

HOME: My first was a grotty flat in Dublin, now I've got a house in London's Chelsea.

HOLIDAYS: Ibiza — it's a great place.

FOOD: Sussex pond pudding.

DRINK: Full bodied dry red wine.

MUSIC: Van Morrison and Prince.

Pop's Mr Scruffy tries to stop the camera catching another unshaven morning, but he's too late

FIRST RECORD: 'Good Vibrations' by the Beach Boys.

FILMS: I loved both *Godfather* movies and *Apocalypse Now*.

HOBBIES: Reading, art, and watching boxing matches. My favourites are Mike Tyson and Barry McGuigan, they are tremendously exciting to watch in action.

ADMIRES: Paula Yates.

HATES: Cynicism.

MOST FRIGHTENING MOMENT: I came pretty close to death when I was in a boat which sank in Italy. And I also survived a nasty motorbike crash when I ran into a wall when I was sixteen. I also have a lasting fear of swimming in public places because I am a terrible swimmer.

FIRST KISS: Her name was Mary O'Dwyer and she was the daughter of a local hotelier. I suddenly felt an inexplicable surge of passion and emotion and we did some energetic kissing. It was pretty pleasant. My first real girlfriend was called Anne Burne. My most memorable early encounter would have been when I was ten at my eldest sister's wedding. My brother-in-law's sister kissed me!

FIRST SEXUAL EXPERIENCE: I was thirteen and she was an older woman of thirty-two who lived down the road from me in Dublin, and yes, it was good for me.

KYLIE MINOGUE

FULL NAME: Kylie Ann Minogue.

BORN: 28/5/1968. Taurus. Melbourne, Australia.

HEIGHT: 5ft 1in.

NICKNAMES: I had the nickname 'Shortie' because I wasn't very big, and they called me 'Bruiser' on the set of 'Neighbours' after I decked Jason Donovan by mistake! I was supposed to punch him in the face but I overdid it and knocked him out. He laughed about it later.

SCHOOL: I wasn't really clever but I was usually too scared to do anything really naughty. I was a bit of a goody-goody but I did cheat off this boy I fancied at school. It was a spelling test and I didn't know how to spell so I copied his answers down. The fear of being caught was terrible!

FIRST JOB: I worked behind the counter of a video shop, earning about £2 a day.

INTO THE BIZ: Through my mum. She encouraged me and my sister Danni from the start and has supported us ever since.

FIRST PERFORMANCE: My very first TV role was a bit-part in a series called 'Skyways'. It was a case of blink and you would have missed me. It was a dreadful show. After that I landed the part of a Dutch girl called Clara in an Australian soap called 'The Sullivans'. I had to speak with a Dutch accent which I wasn't very good at.

MOST NERVE-WRACKING EXPERIENCE: Getting married to Jason on 'Neighbours' was fairly scary because we both knew how much interest there was in the wedding around the world. But I think going topless for my first film *The Delinquents* was the most nerve-wracking experience I've had. I wasn't embarrassed about it, but I was worried that people would get the wrong idea. I was very glad that most critics gave me a good review for the film.

BIGGEST COCK-UP: My suitcase got lost in transit flying to Australia. I was supposed to be on TV and it was a Sunday so I couldn't buy anything. In the end I wore the top of a swimsuit tucked into jeans that I bought from the hotel shop. I felt terrible going on TV looking like that but they all thought I was really trendy!

CAR: I drive an Australian Ford which gets me about easily enough.

HOLIDAYS: Anywhere where it's hot and there is water, like Hawaii or the Caribbean.

Especially for you — rock's most talked about couple Kylie Minogue and INXS singer Michael Hutchence stroll hand in hand from the Orient Express

HOME: My first home was in Melbourne and now I have my own place there. It's Victorian and I really enjoy doing it up.

FOOD: Prawns and anything else that's fishy. I also like spinach, rice puddings, and kiwi fruit.

DRINK: Orange juice — I like having the odd alcoholic drink but it makes me feel sick if I have too much.

MUSIC: I'm really into Soul II Soul, Bobby Brown and Prince.

FIRST RECORD: Abba's *Greatest Hits* — I loved them. I used to have pretend Abba concerts in my bedroom with my friends. I'd prance about pretending to be Agnetha, the blonde one.

FAVE RECORD: 'Sexual Healing' by Marvin Gaye.

FILM: *Terms of Endearment.* I cry every time I watch it. I'm always sobbing over movies.

ADMIRES: Olivia Newton-John because she put Australia on the map. I would like to be like Olivia.

FANCIES: Prince is sex on a stick as far as I am concerned. I have always fancied him.

HOBBIES: Dress-making, horse riding, tenpin bowling and swimming.

HATES: People calling me a star — I could be a nobody tomorrow. And cold weather and my teeth. Rude people — especially people who walk up to me and kiss me without even asking.

Can you spot the superstar? Kylie Minogue (middle row, left) looks even more squeaky clean as a six-year-old pupil than she did as 'Neighbours' star Charlene

WILDEST PARTY: My twenty-first birthday party in Melbourne
FIRST KISS: A boy in second grade. He was really pretty and it was good because there was this really tough girl there who fancied him too, so she would hang around with me to be near him. That gave me a good bodyguard. I wouldn't know him now if I tripped over him!

Jason Donovan

FULL NAME: Jason Sean Donovan. My mum Sue called me Jason after *Jason and the Argonauts* because she had read the poem and fallen in love with him!
BORN: 1/6/1968. Gemini. Melbourne, Australia.
HEIGHT: 5ft 11ins.
NICKNAME: 'Dono', 'Jase', 'Jay'.
SCHOOL: I was pretty average. My best subjects were politics and economics. My worst was accounting. I got the strap once for swinging on some pales. And I cheated quite a lot — though never in a proper exam. I was in the swimming team for two years and played soccer. I wanted to be a graphic designer but kept failing the exams. I was a pretty naughty kid — I remember me and some mates got some dog mess, put it into a brown paper bag and left it on a neighbour's doorstep. We lit the bag, rang the doorbell, and the guy came out, stamped out the flames and got the mess all over him. I also got caught shoplifting when me and my mates nicked stuff from our local newsagent. We were let off and I didn't do it again.
FIRST JOB: I worked in a newsagent's, helping behind the counter and delivering newspapers.
INTO THE BIZ: My mum and dad were established stars already so they were a tremendous inspiration to me. I wanted to be like them.
FIRST PERFORMANCE: It was in a school play called *Trial by Jury*, then at the age of eleven I got a part in a TV show called 'Skyways', which was where I met Kylie Minogue. I was so tubby then — I looked like a little fat-faced ball with a dreadful basin hair-cut.
MOST NERVE-WRACKING EXPERIENCE: Singing live for the first time in front of a crowd about two years ago. I am not the world's greatest singer, and it scared

me stupid. Luckily, I've improved a bit since then. I also remember being trapped in a lift with Kylie when we went to an awards ceremony at a Melbourne hotel. I get claustrophobia so it was pretty scary for me.

GREATEST MOMENT: My first tour was exciting, so was winning a *TV Week* Logie award in Australia. But I guess my best moment would have been landing the role of Scott in 'Neighbours' — that set me up.

BIGGEST COCK-UP: Having my ear pierced when I was a teenager. It seemed like the trendy thing to do at the time — but I don't ever want to wear one again!

CARS: My first was a Golf, now I drive a Range Rover.

HOMES: My first was a two-bedroom home in Melbourne, now a two-bedroom flat in London which I bought last year.

HOLIDAYS: Hawaii — I love going there to surf, especially on a little island called Maui. I always stay in the Hyatt Hotel, where you can watch dolphins playing in the water. I also like Bali.

FOOD: Fried camembert cheese — it's delicious.

DRINK: Fresh orange juice by the gallon.

MUSIC: I like listening to anything that's melodic — especially Paul McCartney and the Beatles. They were brilliant. I like John Farnham and I'm a huge fan of Kiss, Madonna, INXS and Rick Astley.

FIRST RECORD: *Abbey Road* by the Beatles.

FAVE RECORD: My box set of the Beatles albums.

FILM: *Fatal Attraction.* My favourite actor is Michael Douglas. I also like Jack Nicholson, Michael Fox and Meryl Streep.

Twelve-year-old Jason Donovan (middle, with stick) flashes that mischievous smile that has won the hearts of Britain's teenagers ever since

Strewth mate! What a beaut Christmas this has turned out to be. Jason Donovan celebrates another load of presents with Dad Terry

HOBBIES: Swimming, running, playing music, painting and sketching, diving and skiing. But my favourite is surfing. I love getting up before dawn and surfing in Melbourne's beaches when they are deserted. I once was good enough to enter championships but never won anything. A mate of mine is now one of Australia's top surfers. But I remember a very frightening time when I saw shadows in the water while I was paddling out to surf. I thought they were sharks, but then they leapt out of the water and I realised they were dolphins. I almost cried with relief.

ADMIRES: Peter Gabriel — he's a great idol of mine. I've got all his albums.

AMBITION: To be happy and content with my private life and to enjoy my professional life.

HATES: Rude people and traffic — they normally come together. I also hate being in a confined space and wearing shoes!

FANCIES: Meryl Street and Jodie Foster.

MOST FRIGHTENING MOMENT: I was in Los Angeles on holiday and taking a taxi when suddenly this truck came careering towards us out of control. Its brakes had failed and it smashed into the car in front, killing the three people in it. Another couple of feet and I could have been killed too. I also remember a flight from France last year when I looked out of the window to see another plane directly above us. I have done a lot of flying and it was dangerously close. But the airline authorities later denied everything and blamed me for making it up. I'm telling you now — that plane should not have been there and it scared the hell out of me.

WILDEST PARTY: My twenty-first birthday party in Melbourne was pretty wild.

FIRST KISS: I used to play kiss-chase in the school playground a lot — that's how I got my first girlfriend. She was called Kelly, I was about fifteen and she was fourteen.

FIRST SEXUAL EXPERIENCE: I was seventeen and my step-mum Marlene walked into the sitting-room and caught me sowing my wild oats. It was rather embarrassing. I can't remember it too well. But it must have been good because I haven't stopped since — in a caring and sharing way, of course. Being the red-blooded Aussie male that I am, it's only natural!

CRAIG MCLACHLAN

FULL NAME: Craig McLachlan.

BORN: 1/9/1965. Virgo. Sydney, Australia.

HEIGHT: 6ft.

SCHOOL: I left school at sixteen with hardly any qualifications. One report to my mum said: 'If Craig spent as much time studying as he did in the music room he would be a brain surgeon.'

FIRST JOBS: Stocking shelves in a Sydney supermarket, body-building coach, labourer and plumber. I also appeared in TV ads for McDonald's.

INTO THE BIZ: At sixteen I formed a band with my best friend Mark Bain. We called ourselves the Y-Frontz but later changed it to Check 1-2 for obvious reasons.

FIRST PERFORMANCE: It was at the annual school dance and I performed cover versions of the Top 40 hits of the day. I was ten then.

MOST NERVE-WRACKING EXPERIENCE: When I thought I had throat cancer two years ago. I found this lump in my throat but it turned out to be a thyroid gland cyst. In moments like that you realise how important it is to be healthy. That is why I work so hard at keeping fit.

Lady In Red — Yazz looks stunning as she plays another great show

*Especially For You — topless Jason Donovan
shows the muscle that get the girls screaming*

He's a lean, mean fighting machine — soulman
Bobby Brown

Daryl Hall and John Oates one of rock's most
famous duos

Phil Collins at the première of his movie Buster —
with the real-life train robber Buster Edwards
and Julie Walters

Miami Nice — stunning Gloria Estefan turns on the style

Kim Wilde's most embarrassing moment was when her boob popped out on stage — and she nearly repeats it here

Belinda Carlisle used to make ice-cubes out of urine — here she just sings!

*Jazzie B in action — The Soul II Soul maestro
looks super-cool in yellow*

David Bowie on his last major tour

GREATEST MOMENT: Having a number three hit in Britain with my first record 'Mona'.

BIGGEST COCK-UP: I was the prize in a blind date competition in Melbourne. The winners got to date a 'Neighbours' star. Me and Guy Pearce, who played Mike, went out with these two girls and it was so embarrassing. They stared at us for three hours and made it quite clear they expected more than just a peck on the cheek. We both made our excuses and left!

CARS: First car was a battered old Toyota Corolla — now I've got a Jeep and a new Toyota Supra.

HOMES: First home was a house on the beach in Sydney — now I've got my own place there.

HOLIDAYS: Bali is a great place — I would like to go there for my honeymoon when I marry my fiancée Rachel Friend.

FOOD: Pasta — I love Italian food. Ice cream, chocolate and cola.

DRINK: Mineral water without benzene — I'm not a drinker really, it gives me terrible hangovers.

MUSIC: Rock and roll — I love the Stones. I would die to be in the same room as Mick Jagger. And I love Luciano Pavarotti and Mariah Carey. But my all-time heroes would have to be Kiss.

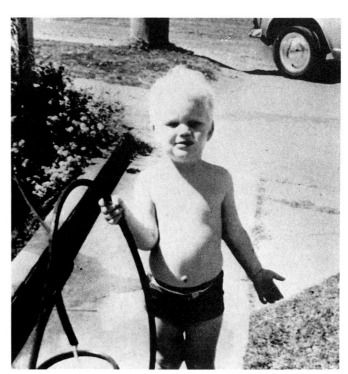

Hey Craig, where are your clothes? A very young McLachlan looks puzzled in his first topless photo

FIRST RECORD: *Jesus Christ Superstar* soundtrack.

FAVE RECORD: 'Start Me Up' by the Rolling Stones.

FILM: *Captain Cabbage Takes Manhattan.*

HOBBIES: Weight-training and keeping fit, and fossil foraging — I'm really into that.

ADMIRES: Kylie Minogue — she's put up with all the pressure and come through it brilliantly. I love her music and she's a great girl.

AMBITION: To run for president in the next US elections.

HATES: Mowing the lawn — especially when you run over your own foot.

FANCIES: Rachel Friend — that's why I am marrying her!

MOST FRIGHTENING MOMENT: I remember the first gig I played after I had been in 'Neighbours' a while. It was a nightmare. It was in a really rough Sydney pub and all these heavy bikers were there. As I walked on they started chanting: 'Henry is a poofter, poofter.' I felt awful. But by the end of the show they were enjoying themselves.

WILDEST PARTY: The Baronis Netball Association presentation and trophy night. I was guest of honour and it was wild!

FIRST KISS: Her name was Ethel and I was ten. She had braces and bunches. When she told me she wanted our relationship to progress past kissing I was terrified.

FIRST SEXUAL EXPERIENCE: I was anxious, scared, excited, nervous and alone!

Yes that is a bra on your head! Craig McLachlan suffering another attack from an admiring female

Bobby Brown

FULL NAME: Bobby Berisford Brown.

BORN: 5/2/1969. Aquarius. Boston, Massachusetts.

HEIGHT: 5ft 10ins.

NICKNAMES: 'Bobby' or 'Bob'.

SCHOOL: I left in 1981 or 82. I had a tutor for the rest of the time. I would not describe myself as one of life's great students.

INTO THE BIZ: I used to jam in the streets with my friends — I pretended I was Stevie Wonder or Michael Jackson.

FIRST PERFORMANCE: I was three and James Brown got me up on stage during one of his shows to dance with him because I was down the front of the stage. I loved it in front of all those people.

MOST NERVE-WRACKING EXPERIENCE: When my daughter was being born — I was in the hospital room. And I am always nervous at awards shows before my peers.

GREATEST MOMENT: Accepting the People's Choice award in February 1990. It felt so good standing there and knowing that thousands of people had voted for me.

BIGGEST COCK-UP: I fell off the stage in London singing 'Every Little Step' would you believe? It was a drop of about 10ft and I got back onto the stage feeling so embarrassed. It proved that every little step does count.

CARS: My first was a Maximum. Now I have seven cars — three Mercedes, two Jeeps, a Jaguar and a BMW.

HOME: I built a big home in Atlanta.

HOLIDAYS: Christmas because I love giving gifts. I like going to London especially, it's like a second home to me.

FOOD: Seafood — I don't eat beef or pork.

DRINK: I like a beer but prefer water.

MUSIC: Stevie Wonder is my hero — and Janet Jackson.

FIRST RECORD: 'Grandmaster Flash' by the Message.

FAVE RECORD: Greatest hits of Donny Hathaway.

FILM: I watch them all but if I could have only one video it would be *Casablanca*.

HOBBIES: Weight–lifting, boxing.

ADMIRES: I admire people who work hard to succeed.

AMBITION: I would like to act and write, and try everything in the entertainment business.

HATES: None really, I am not a hateful person.

FANCIES: My heart belongs to Janet Jackson.

MOST FRIGHTENING MOMENT: I was shot in the knee when I was ten. I got caught up in a domestic dispute and it hurt! I also got stabbed a few times in street fights when I was a teenager.

WILDEST PARTY: I had some pretty wild nights when I was a teenager. I remember one where gate-crashers burst in and threatened to shoot everyone. That was hairy, man.

FIRST KISS: I was seven years old and it was my baby-sitter. I ain't joking. She was fifteen, and I came on to her. I had been watching the moves of my older brother.

FIRST SEXUAL EXPERIENCE: I was twelve years old and it was with my daughter's mother. It was a memorable experience.

Soul superstar Bobby Brown in typically flamboyant hat and chains but you'd think all that money would make him smile

CURT SMITH

FULL NAME: Curt Smith.

BORN: 24/6/1961. Cancer. Bath, Avon.

HEIGHT: 5ft 8ins.

NICKNAME: 'Mr Fish' is the name I use for booking into hotels on tour. Unfortunately, some fans got to know this so I keep getting fish gifts — fish socks, ties, etc. It's a real pain in the neck!

SCHOOL: I was good at most things but I dropped out after getting seven O–levels to go into music full time.

FIRST JOBS: I had lots of part-time jobs, like window cleaning and clearing shelves in a Gateway supermarket. All very interesting . . .

INTO THE BIZ: I joined Roland's band called the Graduate.

FIRST SHOW: I was thirteen and it was with Roland's group which had been re-named Cobra by then. We did cover versions of Thin Lizzy songs. We were fairly awful.

MOST NERVE-WRACKING EXPERIENCE: I was incredibly nervous before the Nelson Mandela show. It was just the fear of performing in front of one billion people! But once we got going it was great — an amazing day.

GREATEST MOMENT: Going to number one in America was fantastic. We were filming a video that day and I was so knackered I had fallen asleep! Then someone woke me up and told me I was number one — we partied until very late that night!

BIGGEST COCK-UP: I am always falling over. I fell over on stage twice during the last tour and once during a foreign TV interview. The first time was the worst. I came running out on stage, tripped on a cable and slid across the stage on dry ice — right off the end. I sat there for five seconds thinking, how am I going to get out of this? Then I got up and carried on. I think some people thought it was part of the act.

CARS: I had a Mini and a Fiat Panda. I now have a red 1959 Triumph TR3.

HOMES: I had a four-bedroom rectory in North Wrexall, near Bath, but I've just sold it. I've got two homes, one in Chelsea, London and a loft in the Soho district of New York.

HOLIDAYS: Anywhere hot. The best holiday I have had was in Grenada in the West Indies. The people were so friendly.

FOOD: I love food, and my favourite cuisine is probably French. I love the Ménage à Trois restaurant in Beauchamp Place, London, and the China Grill in New York.

DRINK: I like white wine.

MUSIC: Not really pop, more R and B, jazz and classical. My favourite singers are Donald Fagin and Bette Midler.

FIRST RECORD: *Slade Alive* — great album!

FAVE RECORD: Peter Gabriel's third album.

FILM: *Being There* starring Peter Sellers.

HOBBIES: I have leaned to fly, and have my helicopter pilot's licence. And I like racing saloon cars — very yuppie I know.

ADMIRES: Soul II Soul and De La Soul.

AMBITION: To be happy in life and to try acting. I am a big film fan.

HATES: Tomatoes.

FANCIES: Darryl Hannah, she's lovely.

MOST FRIGHTENING MOMENT: When I am a passenger in a car, I cling to doors and press imaginary air brakes. I hate it when I'm not doing the driving.

WILDEST PARTY: I have had so many to be honest, especially when I had my house in Bath. It had an outdoor pool which I would heat to ninety degrees! That was pretty damn wild then.

FIRST KISS: I was five and she was a little girl called Karen Jones who lived two doors away from me. Nothing serious. First girlfriend was Cheryl at junior school when I was ten.

FIRST SEXUAL EXPERIENCE: It was in Wales in a caravan. I was about fourteen and on a camping trip with ten mates. It was quite boring and I found out later that it helps if you are in love. She was two years older and more experienced than me. I don't think I even asked her her name. I met her in a club.

Tears for Fears singer Curt Smith has no reason for either tears or fears, he has become one of the biggest stars in the world

Yazz

REAL NAME: Yasmin Marie Evans.

BORN: 19/5/1960. Taurus. Shepherd's Bush, West London.

HEIGHT: 5ft 11ins.

NICKNAME: 'Hotlips' because of my red lipstick.

SCHOOL: I played volleyball for the England under-19s and won loads of medals. I've got very long legs and the 400 metres was my forte. I enjoyed arts and drama but not the rest.

FIRST JOBS: I worked in a hairdressing salon in Shepherd's Bush as a Saturday job, rinsing old ladies' hair. I was terrible and I used to turn lots of the old dears' hair blue depending on how nice they were to me. I also did a lot of modelling to make money to finance studio time.

INTO THE BIZ: I was a late starter and only got into pop in my early twenties with a band called Pastiche, but I didn't have a clue. I wore clogs and had a huge Afro, absolutely massive. It wafted up and down when I walked down the street. Then we met Jazz Summers and he agreed to manage us. I later married him.

Yazz laughs at another glittering party — and why not? She has had a great career so far

MOST NERVE-WRACKING EXPERIENCE: My first appearance on 'Top of the Pops'. I thought I was Whitney Houston! It was terrifying but great.

GREATEST MOMENT: The birth of my baby daughter Rio and my first live gig in a 2000-seater cow-shed in Dublin in April 1989.

BIGGEST COCK-UP: I forgot the lyrics to 'Only Way is Up' at the Hammersmith Odeon. It was especially awful because it was in London. I ummed and ooed for about three minutes, but it felt like an eternity. It was so embarrassing. The band were loving it. I don't think the audience realised what was happening.

HOME: I live in Camden, North London in a first floor flat.

HOLIDAYS: Jamaica, definitely.

FOOD: Pasta, a big fan.

DRINK: Champagne — Veuve Clicquot like James Bond.

MUSIC: David Sanbourne, soft jazz and Bill Franks. My favourite singers are Stevie Wonder, Marvin Gaye and Suzanne Vega.

FIRST RECORD: 'Ain't No Mountain High Enough' by the Supremes.

FAVE RECORD: 'What's Going On' by Marvin Gaye.

FILM: *Now Voyager* starring Bette Davis.

HOBBIES: Sport and learning to drive.

ADMIRES: Bruce Webber, a US photographer who does nude work. I would love to sit for him though not in the nude. And Nelson Mandela.

AMBITION: I wanted a natural birth and I had one. That was my biggest ambition. My baby was born naturally on the floor. I would also like a small cameo part in a film.

HATES: Spiders, sycophants and scrambled eggs.

FANCIES: Prince for his charisma and body, Michael Hutchence — though his taste in women recently has put me off — and John Sachs of course!

MOST FRIGHTENING MOMENT: I saw a lot of drug addicts shooting up in New York and one of them died. It scared me stupid and put me off drugs for life.

WILDEST PARTY: My next birthday party will be wild.

FIRST KISS: I was thirteen, he was called Michael and it was in the school cloakroom behind all the coats and stuff. Horrible, nought out of ten rating — if that! It was all wet and wishy washy, bless him. My first boyfriend was Ben who I worked with in a club when I was seventeen. We were together for a few years and it was really nice until I got bored.

FIRST SEXUAL EXPERIENCE: It was wonderful, absolutely wonderful. I was twenty-one, a late developer. He was a bit older. I was petrified. He was a damn good lover! He has nothing to do with this business and I'm not telling you his name.

PAULA ABDUL

FULL NAME: Paula Julie Abdul.

BORN: 19/6/1963. Gemini. Los Angeles, California.

HEIGHT: 5ft 2ins.

NICKNAMES: 'P' or 'Peedee' since school. I prefer Paula!

SCHOOL: I remember falling down a manhole when I was at school. I wasn't looking where I was going because I was concentrating on a big exam. The most amazing thing about my childhood was that my baby-sitter when I was seven years old was a certain Michael Bolton! We have a good laugh about it now — I seem to recall that he fancied my sister.

FIRST JOBS: I worked in a really trendy clothes shop called Contempo Casuals in the evenings after school when I was about fourteen. Then when I was sixteen I worked in a restaurant as a part-time waitress.

INTO THE BIZ: I auditioned to be a Laker girl for the Los Angeles Lakers. I choreographed the team because I didn't like doing all that ra-ra stuff. I met Jack Nicholson, McEnroe, Huey Lewis, and the Jackson Five. The latter asked me to work with them because they were so impressed.

FIRST PERFORMANCE: In a school production of *Grease* when I was ten and I did ballet classes six days a week from the age of six.

GREATEST MOMENT: Going number one in America with 'Straight Up' and having raging 'flu with a 103 degree temperature at the time! I was as sick as a dog and couldn't celebrate. Prince sent me a telegram, Michael Jackson rang to say well done and Luther Vandross sent me the biggest bunch of flowers I have ever seen.

MOST NERVE-WRACKING EXPERIENCE: I was robbed while I was at the MTV awards. They took thousands of pounds worth of jewellery including some irreplaceable stuff that belonged to my mum. In all they took about £26,000 worth.

CAR: Black Jaguar XJS convertible.

HOME: I live in West Hollywood. And the house has murals all over the walls. My pets include Rambo, a chihuahua, a pug called Pebbles and a cocker spaniel called Sadie.

FOOD: I like vegetables and fruit, chicken and fish. My dad used to be a meat-packer so I don't like meat much. My favourite meal is pasta which I cook brilliantly!

Paula Abdul sings that opposites attract
and they are queuing up to be opposite
her

MUSIC: I'm into most things — Michael and Janet Jackson, George Michael, Cher.

FILMS: I loved *Singing in the Rain, Oliver!* and *Saturday Night Fever.* I worked with John Travolta last year and he was asking me for dance lessons. He's got a great grin, though. I like Patrick Swayze too.

FIRST RECORD: 'I Want you Back' by the Jacksons.

HOBBIES: I like bike-riding. I often go with my sister for thirty-mile rides to my nearest beach. I'm dead by the time I get back though.

ADMIRES: Gene Kelly — I love the man. I've seen all his films and when I finally met him I was sweating with fear. I was a nervous wreck. I just told him I loved him and could I give him a hug! Now we are really good friends and I see him for tea virtually every week.

MOST FRIGHTENING MOMENT: I was hit by a drunk driver. I was driving along the freeway at eleven p.m. and I could see this car behind me swinging from side to side. I realised he was drunk. He just ploughed into me, I hit another car and was spun round to face the oncoming traffic. I was then hit by another car; six cars were smashed in the accident. I woke up in hospital and was lucky to have survived the crash.

FIRST CRUSH: In fifth grade. He was the tallest kid in the class and called Dan — he was so cute but stood out like a sore thumb. It was a crush though, and the last time I heard of him he was thinking of running for president!

Janet Jackson

FULL NAME: Janet Damita Jackson.

BORN: 16/5/1966. Taurus. Gary, Indiana.

HEIGHT: 5ft 2ins.

NICKNAME: Michael calls me 'Dunce'.

SCHOOL: I was a pretty good student.

FIRST JOB: I worked as a papergirl for about £1 a week.

INTO THE BIZ: I took my first piano lessons when I was about seven. I didn't do it for very long because my brothers were so much better than me. Randy in particular is brilliant on the keyboards.

FIRST PERFORMANCE: I appeared with my brothers on the 'Jackson's Summer

Special' in 1973. I was seven years old and it was in Las Vegas — I was scared stiff.

MOST NERVE-WRACKING EXPERIENCE: When I saw Michael's head on fire after a bomb exploded on him while he was making a Pepsi advert. Everyone else thought it was part of the commercial except me. I screamed: 'Mikey, Mikey, oh baby' and ran over to him. He was just lying on the ground kicking, and there was this huge bald patch on his head. I started to cry.

GREATEST MOMENT: Playing in New York at the start of my first major solo tour. There were thousands of fans screaming my name — that was a magical moment.

BIGGEST COCK-UP: When I accidentally flashed my knickers in front of the Queen during the Royal Command Performance. I heard my skirt rip and I just wanted to die. I was also embarrassed when my pet panther Rhythm urinated on stage in America. I had been using him throughout the tour and this was the first time he had done it. I slid on it, and fell straight over. When I got up I had this embarrassing wet patch on my bum.

CARS: I've got a Mercedes 190E and a Range Rover — it's not the car you drive that matters, it's who is driving it.

HOME: I've recently bought a new house in Del Mar, about 130 miles from Los Angeles. It has six bedrooms and I love it.

HOLIDAYS: I love Egypt and the pyramids. Britain fascinates me — I can spend hours in the British Museum looking at all that history. And I am always going to Disneyland with my friends — it's a great place.

FOOD: I like fish and chicken but do not eat red meat.

DRINK: Water.

MUSIC: I love rock bands like Aerosmith and Def Leppard — I would like to meet Joe Elliott. And I have a lot of respect for Aretha Franklin and Marvin Gaye.

FIRST RECORD: 'Black Dog' by Led Zeppelin.

FAVE RECORD: Anything by Aerosmith or Def Leppard. I'm really into heavy rock.

HOBBIES: I like skinny-dipping in the sea. But I've been caught a few times by fishermen which can be a bit embarrassing. I also like bareback horseriding. I collect pigs — porcelain and stuffed fabric ones. It all started when I used to look after my grandfather's hog on his farm.

FILM: I loved *ET*.

ADMIRES: Fred Astaire — I was a great fan, but now he's dead I will never get the chance to meet him. I also adore Mae West.

AMBITION: To have ten kids and to perform in a stage show on Broadway. I think

Janet Jackson proves that Michael's not the only one who can turn on the style with another sensational stage show

doing a musical would be a tremendous challenge.

HATES: I hate people who ask me what it is like to be Michael Jackson's sister.

FANCIES: The New Kids are lovely — especially Jordan. They are so cute. And I love Steve Tyler from Aerosmith, he's hunky.

MOST FRIGHTENING MOMENT: I was coming out of my bedroom when I saw this strange fat man on the landing. I nearly screamed, I thought it was a burglar. Then he said 'Hi Dunce' and I realized it was my brother Michael. He was wearing one of the many disguises he uses so that he can go out on the streets and preach as a Jehovah's Witness.

FIRST KISS: James De Barge.

FIRST SEXUAL EXPERIENCE: I married James De Barge when I was sixteen and he was the first man I ever made love to. It was wonderful. I had waited until our wedding night because I wanted it to be special. We were in a beautiful hotel by the river and there was a fireworks display going off outside.

JON BON JOVI

REAL NAME: Jon Frank Bon Jovi

BORN: 2/3/1962. Perth, Australia. As an Aries I am supposed to need a good strong woman to kick me up the backside but I've never needed no chick to tell me what to do.

HEIGHT: 5ft 10ins.

NICKNAME: 'Jonjo'.

SCHOOL: I got kicked out of the Holy Rosary kindergarten because I whacked a girl who had a crush on me — she was being a pain in the ass. I always used to say that I was bored and I was. I hated it. I was a bad kid — I was drinking, smoking pot and stealing by the time I was thirteen.

FIRST JOBS: Selling newspaper subscriptions door-to-door, working for Burger King, a car wash and a junkyard. My longest job was for Kinney Shoes where I was told to wear a suit and tie. But my jacket was green, and I wore sunglasses. My boss finally sacked me for turning the radio up whenever Springsteen came on. He said, 'Hey, rock star, you're fired!'

INTO THE BIZ: I picked up a guitar because I wanted to play on the beach and pick up girls. But my first instructor, Al Parinello, told my mum that I was a lousy musician and would never make it. My first band was called Raze.

FIRST PERFORMANCE: At the Stone Pony club. The owner said he would kill us if we didn't go down well — that was a good incentive.

MOST NERVE-WRACKING EXPERIENCE: I took some drugs when I was thirteen and had the most horrendous hallucinations and nightmares. I watched spaghetti crawl across my plate. I was rushed straight to hospital.

GREATEST MOMENT: Playing in Moscow. Everyone warned me about how ugly the chicks were — fat Siberians with moustaches and camouflage suits — but Miss Siberia was a lovely little blonde.

BIGGEST COCK-UP: When I came home with long hair and dad took one look at it and cut it all off! I couldn't go out for weeks, it was so awful. Now he does my hair all the time — but keeps it long.

CARS: My first was a Datsun 280Z. Now I have four cars including a 1969 Camaro and a 1958 Corvette and a Jeep.

HOMES: A two-storey house in Sayreville, New Jersey was the first. Now I live in a ratty one-bed apartment on the Jersey shoreline. It's just somewhere to send the

Jon Bon Jovi may be the best-looking
rocker in town, but that's no way to treat
your beer . . .

mail.
HOLIDAY: Home in New Jersey.
FOOD: Sausage. McMuffins.
DRINK: Tequila slammers.
MUSIC: Springsteen — if you don't buy three Bruce albums a year in New Jersey
you get taxed extra! — and the Grateful Dead.
FIRST RECORD: Bob Dylan's 'Blood on the Tracks'.

FAVE RECORDS: The last Hanoi Rocks album and anything by Billy Idol. 'Bang Bang' by Sonny and Cher — I wished I'd written that.

FILM: *Dirty Harry* — and anything violent.

HOBBIES: Sleeping and eating junk food and pizza, good stuff like that.

ADMIRES: I've been trying to meet Eddie Murphy but he won't return my calls.

AMBITION: To make it through the day. But beyond that I would like to be eating coconuts on a desert island with three or four naked women.

HATES: Travelling is tiresome.

FANCIES: Chicks — all of them.

MOST FRIGHTENING MOMENT: When I was seventeen, I was at a parkway and some guy cut me up in his car so I drove after him real fast. It turned out he was a marshall and before I knew it, I was surrounded at gunpoint. That terrified me! They put me in the slammer for a night.

WILDEST PARTY: The day I got married. I was in Las Vegas, I went to a tattoo parlour, went gambling and won lots of money, got drunk and said 'Hey, let's get married.' So we did — there wasn't even a best man. The next day I woke up and said: 'I did what?'

FIRST KISS: Her name was Bertha. She was tall with red hair, a tattoo, weighed about 400 pounds and she taught me everything I know. I was never very good at pulling the chicks. My first real girlfriend was Adrian Pillar who was at high school with me.

FIRST SEXUAL EXPERIENCE: I was fourteen and she was fifteen. By the time I was her age I was an old man sexually!

Jazzie B

REAL NAME: Berisford Romeo.

BORN: 10/1/1963. Capricorn. Finsbury Park, North London.

HEIGHT: 5ft 10ins.

NICKNAME: 'Jazzie'.

HOBBIES: Buying clothes and training shoes — I've got 250 pairs at the moment.

SCHOOL: I was at Holloway Boys School in North London. I really enjoyed my school days though I was pretty rebellious and always being thrown out of class for being lippy to the teachers. My favourite subject was sociology because it allowed me to talk for hours on end. I loathed physics and chemistry but was mad-keen on football until I damaged my knee and had to stop playing. Cyrille Regis was my hero — he was a London lad from the same background as me.

INTO THE BIZ: I became a club DJ.

FIRST PERFORMANCE: The first live show I did was with Soul II Soul in America — but I had been a DJ for years before that.

MOST NERVE-WRACKING EXPERIENCE: With as many gold teeth as I've got, people think I like dentists but actually I've got a phobia about them. As a youth I had a bad experience with the school dentist. I lost some teeth when I fell off something and the dentist was a bit of a butcher. So now I'm very nervous when I have to go, though I've got someone good who looks after me — my godmother is a dentist. Why gold teeth? It's just vanity, really.

GREATEST MOMENT: Beating Madonna to the top of the album charts. We came out the same week as her and I never dreamed we could beat her to number one. When we did I thought: That's what I call a result! It chuffed me more than anything else.

BIGGEST COCK-UP: I find it incredibly embarrassing when girls come up to me in the street screaming at me. I also get a lot of saucy fan mail which can be quite embarrassing too.

CAR: A Mercedes which I have valeted every week — it's my pride and joy.

HOMES: I live in North London but I also own a fair amount of real estate around Britain. I'm also trying to make a hefty purchase in the Caribbean for my family — if my accountant gets his act together.

HOLIDAYS: Antigua, where my parents come from. I like climbing trees and building fires — that sort of thing.

FOOD: I like spicy food — curries and stuff like that.

MUSIC: I'm into the B52's in a big way. Melba Moore's great, too, and I like a rap band called A.P.R.T. And Madonna's real cool — she's in my red book. She wanted to do a song with us, but we were too busy.

HOBBIES: I like sleeping in the bath. People tell me it's dangerous but I like it. One thing I won't do is smoke a cigar in the bath. I tried it once after watching an episode of 'Bonanza' where they were all smoking cigars in the bath but it was horrible.

ADMIRES: My mum is my best friend and I talk to her every day. I can reason with her about things and I can trust her. She tells me off for going on 'Top of the Pops'. I go round and clean her windows every Christmas with wet newspaper. It's a very cheap, efficient way of doing it.

AMBITION: I am working on building a hospital which takes care of people in our community. You very rarely see black people in a private practice. You have to take care of your own. It will be funded by members of Soul II Soul.

HATES: I can't see the point in spending all that money on sending people to the moon when so much of the world is starving. It's a nonsense.

MOST FRIGHTENING MOMENT: I was in my Soul II Soul shop in Camden, North London by myself and I suddenly felt this presence. Then the drawers and doors started opening of their own accord right in front of me. It was weird, and made me believe in ghosts. Also my first appearance on 'Top of the Pops' was terrifying. I used to watch it with all my mates when I was younger but actually going on it made me scared as I have ever been. I don't think I will go on it again — it's for pop stars like Bros and Lisa Stansfield really, not me.

FANCIES: I like Madonna — she's a sexy lady.

FIRST SEXUAL EXPERIENCE: I've been in love once but it didn't work out. That has made me selfish.

Soul II Soul creator Jazzie B takes a break and he's earned it. Now he is one of the most successful pop names in Britain

PAUL McCARTNEY

FULL NAME: James Paul McCartney.

BORN: 18/7/1942. Gemini. Liverpool.

HEIGHT: 5ft 11ins.

NICKNAME: 'Macca'.

SCHOOL: I loved art and studied it at the Liverpool Institute with Derek Hatton, believe it or not. He used to spend most of his time in detention. My claim to fame was that I could draw naked ladies. I did them on folded paper so that when it was folded the lady had her clothes on and when you unfolded it . . . wey hey! Then my mum found one in my trouser pocket and told my dad to have words. Talk about anguish, it was death, tears.

FIRST JOB: I went down to the local labour exchange and asked for the first job on their sheet. It was sweeping up at a coil-winding factory! They asked me to make coil-winders for £16 a week.

INTO THE BIZ: Dad told me to play the piano because it would get me invites to parties. I met Lennon at the Walton Parish Church fête and joined his band the Quarrymen who were appearing there.

FIRST PERFORMANCE: The very first was at Butlins in Pwllheli in Wales. It was a talent contest and me and my brother sang 'Bye Bye Love'. The first performance with the Beatles was at the Liverpool Conservative club in Woolton which has now been converted into a bus shelter. It was pretty disastrous — I got sticky fingers playing guitar.

MOST NERVE-WRACKING EXPERIENCE: Meeting the Queen when we got the MBEs at the Palace. She was great; asked me where we were playing next and I said it was Slough. She said 'That's near me in Windsor.' I think she was joking.

GREATEST MOMENT: Going to America for the first time with the Beatles and playing to 180,000 fans in Rio on the same tour.

BIGGEST COCK-UP: Not getting hold of the Lennon-McCartney Northern songs when they were up for sale. I told Yoko Ono we could get them for £20 million between us but she said we could get them cheaper. In the end Michael Jackson got them for £55 million.

CARS: The first one was an MG roadster. Now I drive a Mercedes and a Land Rover. I am not really into cars.

HOMES: Scotland, Sussex and Santa Barbara.

HOLIDAYS: My favourite was in Greece when Beatlemania made it the only place I could go where I wouldn't be recognised.

FOOD: Tex-Mex and Linda's veggie quiche that only real men can eat. And cheese and lettuce sarnies with lots of mayonnaise. I still love egg and chips and chip butties, too.

DRINKS: Iced water and Scotch and Coke which I developed a taste for because Ringo Starr used to drink gallons of it. But after four I am anybody's — I can't take my drink.

MUSIC: I own the Buddy Holly catalogue and I liked Elvis before he joined the army, James Brown, the Beach Boys, Chuck Berry and Stevie Wonder.

FAVE RECORDS: 'Sex machine' by James Brown and *Pet Sounds* by the Beach Boys. There wouldn't have been a *Sergeant Pepper* without that Beach Boys album — it was a great influence on us at the time.

HOBBIES: Painting, sailing, writing. I have done 300 paintings in the last three years but I'm not selling them — yet!

FILM: *On the Waterfront* with Marlon Brando.

AMBITION: To make a really good song!

HATES: Bigots, racists, hotels and travelling.

MOST FRIGHTENING EXPERIENCE: There were some very scary times with the Beatles when screaming girls used to crush against the cars. There was always the fear that they might crush us to death!

FIRST KISS: Grace Pendelton — when I was eleven. She was my first girlfriend at Belle Vale school. I went past her house in Speke where I used to live and I saw her navy blue knickers on the washing line. When I told her this, she said: 'Well, at least they were clean and paid for.'

FIRST SEXUAL EXPERIENCE: You cannot be serious.

Do you recognise the chirpy little chap in the back row fourth from left? He went on to form the world's greatest group — it's Paul McCartney

Ex-Beatles stars Paul McCartney and
Ringo Starr celebrate yet more millions
piling in with wives Linda and Barbara

Hall & Oates

DARYL HALL

FULL NAME: Daryl Franklin Hall.

BORN: 10/11/1949. Scorpio. Pennsylvania.

HEIGHT: 5ft 9ins.

NICKNAME: 'Sinclair'. It's the name I use when I am staying in hotels.

SCHOOL: I was the classic juvenile delinquent. I got pretty good grades but I was always in trouble.

Daryl Hall, half of one of the biggest double acts in the business

FIRST JOB: I earned 50p an hour working in an apple orchard.

INTO THE BIZ: I sang on stage from the age of three.

FIRST PERFORMANCE: It was at Hecate Circle in Philadelphia in 1970. It went great; we played mainly traditional stuff.

BIGGEST COCK-UP: I remember my piano collapsing on stage during a show and the roadie point blank refusing to come out and fix it. Luckily, a fan leaped on stage, and fixed the piano. I hired him as a roadie and sacked the other guy.

CARS: I bought a 1968 Dodge Charger which I had to give back after six months because I couldn't afford the repayments. Now I have a couple of Jeeps, two tractors and two motorbikes.

HOMES: My first was in Connecticut, now I live in New York.

HOLIDAYS: St. Barts in the Caribbean, it's breathtakingly beautiful.

FOOD: Italian.

DRINK: Real ale.

MUSIC: David Ruffin or Marvin Gaye would be favourite.

FIRST RECORD: 'It's Gonna Work out Fine' by Ike and Tina Turner.

FILM: *Batman* and *Pink Flamingoes*.

HOBBIES: Reading and hunting.

HATES: Being manipulated and being told what is best for me by people who don't know.

FANCIES: Charlotte Rampling.

FIRST KISS: Her name was Susan and it was in the back of the school bus. Literally two seconds after I kissed her the bus crashed! I suppose you could say the earth moved.

FIRST SEXUAL EXPERIENCE: I was fifteen and she was twelve. Her name was Kathy and she was very well developed for her age. It all happened in her parents' basement in the heart of the ghetto in Pennsylvania. It was great — I was so pleased to finally do it.

JOHN OATES

FULL NAME: John William Oates.
BORN: 4/7/1948. Cancer. New York, New York.
NICKNAME: I don't really have one.
SCHOOL: I stood out at school because it was full of tall, blond Germans and I was the complete opposite.
FIRST JOB: I was about four years old when I got my first pay packet — £3 for singing with a band on a bar-room stage in New York.
MOST NERVE-WRACKING EXPERIENCE: When Daryl and I got held up by an armed robber in a restaurant in Melbourne, Australia. He had a sawn-off shotgun and was known as the 'Rusty Gun Bandit' because he had an old gun and had committed a lot of robberies. It was just us and the waiters so we decided we had to go for it. We pushed him through a plate glass widow, and he was arrested. The funniest thing was that I was sitting under a picture of Ned Kelly when he broke in!
CARS: I bought a Volvo 244 with Daryl in 1969. It was very old and eventually caught fire after three years. Now I've got quite a large collection including a Toyota, a Jeep, an E-type Jag, a Porche, and a 1955 Chevvy convertible.
HOME: I bought my first real home in Connecticut in 1983.
HOLIDAYS: I love skiing, so I will go anywhere there is snow.
FOOD: Italian.

John Oates, the other half of one of the world's great double acts

DRINK: Clean water.
MUSIC: My all-time favourite is Little Richard.
FIRST RECORD: 'Johnny B. Goode' by Chuck Berry.
FILM: *Batman*.
HOBBIES: Cycling, skiing.
HATES: I hate narrow-minded people.
FANCIES: Brigitte Bardot — she is gorgeous.
FIRST KISS: It was with a friend's sister behind a barn. I was twelve, she was fourteen.
FIRST SEXUAL EXPERIENCE: I was cruising through town with a friend when I was sixteen. We picked up this girl and had a lot of wine and one thing led to another. It ended up with both me and my mate Rebel losing our virginity — one after the other. She was very experienced — and very keen! But I don't recall it was one of my better performances — in fact, it was terrible.

BELINDA CARLISLE

FULL NAME: Belinda Jo Carlisle.
BORN: 17/8/1958. Leo. Hollywood, California.
HEIGHT: 5ft 5ins.
NICKNAMES: 'B' and 'BC'.
SCHOOL: Bret Heart in Burbank, California. I never applied myself and never cared. I graduated at seventeen. I had an athletic scholarship, in track. That was about all I was really good at.
FIRST JOBS: I scooped ice cream, worked in a fabric store, was a secretary, and a petrol pump attendant.
INTO THE BIZ: I formed a punk band called the Germs, and then in 1978 formed the Go-Gos with some mates.
FIRST PERFORMANCE: With the Go-Gos at the Rock Corporation, California.
MOST NERVE-WRACKING EXPERIENCE: Playing Madison Square Garden with the Go-Gos. I couldn't get the first three songs out — I was so scared seeing all those people. I was just standing there moving my lips and nothing was coming out. I couldn't believe it — then suddenly a noise came out and I was away!

She has been through drink, drugs and
man problems but former Go-Gos star
Belinda Carlisle has come out of it looking
great

GREATEST MOMENT: Opening for the Rolling Stones with the Go-Gos at
Rockford, Illinois. And going number one with 'Heaven on Earth'.

BIGGEST COCK-UP: I wore spiked heels on stage, caught my skirt and pulled it
off in front of 15,000 people. It was so embarrassing. I had underwear on but it
was terrible. The biggest mistake of my life was doing drugs.

CARS: My first was a 1967 Plymouth Satellite. Now I have a Mercedes Jeep.

HOMES: First was a two-bedroom house in California. Now I live in a house built for Carole Lombard in 1937 in the Canyon area of LA. It's quaint, but grand.

HOLIDAYS: Thanksgiving is my favourite time of the year. And I love the South of France.

FOOD: Mexican.

DRINKS: Tequila and Margarita.

MUSIC: I love Texas R and B music. And my favourite singer is Chrissie Hynde — she has so much talent.

FIRST RECORDS: Bobby Sherman, 'Hey Little Woman' and 'Aquarius' by Destination.

FAVE RECORD: Pretenders, The Singles.

FILM: *La Dolce Vita* by Fellini.

HOBBIES: Gardening and relaxing.

AMBITION: To make more great songs.

HATES: Beetroot and cruelty to animals. Fur coats.

WILDEST PARTY: I would say it was the Go-Gos and INXS tour in the States. It lasted six weeks, pretty well non-stop.

FIRST KISS: I was thirteen, we played Truth or Dare and the guy never talked to me afterwards. He was the same age, and his name was Jack Wild. My first boyfriend was Carlos from the Dickies when I was eighteen.

Terence Trent D'Arby

REAL NAME: Terence Trent Darby. Trent is actually my middle name, and I added the apostrophe to make my surname more pretentious.

BORN: 16/3/1962. Pisces. Manhattan, New York City.

NICKNAME: They call me 'T' to my face.

SCHOOL: We moved to Daytona Beach, Florida when I was two. I enjoyed break time because they used to have milk in giant cartons and I loved it. My first grade teacher Miss Griffin had twin sons in my class and she was very matronly. I remember her vividly.

FIRST JOBS: My first job was as a landscape gardener with a bunch of mates, raking leaves and moving lawns, etc. Then I worked in McDonald's frying hamburgers. Then I joined the army in America and Germany. I boxed, and was not bad. They said I had lots of potential but never realised it fully. I reached the rank of corporal and would have been a sergeant but I quit for music.

FIRST PERFORMANCE: In Germany with a small group called Simplicity. I was the percussionist.

GREATEST MOMENT: The birth of my daughter Seraphina at Portland Hospital was brilliant. Also meeting Nelson Mandela and Jessie Jackson on the day of the Mandela show.

Terence Trent D'Arby may be a legend in his own mind, but he records great music

BIGGEST COCK-UP: I was beaten up by a girl after school when I was eleven. She was older and bigger and gave me a right beating! It was humiliating. Everyone gathered round and watched and jeered me. I had to live with that for the rest of my school days.

CAR: My first car was a '66 Ford Mustang fastback which my dad bought me for graduating. I don't drive any more, I prefer riding a bike.

HOMES: Manhattan was the first. I've lived in London since 1986.

HOLIDAYS: I spend a lot of time in Italy and I am thinking of settling down there. Also Ireland and Jamaica.

FOOD: Brown rice.

DRINK: Water — any brand so long as it is clear.

MUSIC: I like Beethoven, Prince, the Rolling Stones, Hank Williams.

FIRST RECORD: 'I Want you Back' by the Jackson Five.

SINGERS: Sam Cooke, Sinatra, Otis Redding, Tony Bennett, Aretha Franklin, Nat King Cole and Shirley Bassey.

FILMS: *Amadeus,* I've seen it ten times, twice a year at least! And I loved *Raging Bull* and anything by Woody Allen.

HOBBIES: Scuba diving, riding my Harley Davidson.

ADMIRES: Mickey Rourke, Robert De Niro, Pete Townsend, Michael Jackson, Chrissie Hynde, Prince.

AMBITION: To direct films and write film scores. I am losing interest in pop and will be taking a break after this album. I would like to do string quartets.

HATES: Closed-minded bigots, cynical and mean-spirited people.

WILDEST PARTIES: In the recording studio making the last album at Hook End Manor. My birthday party in Berkshire near Henley.

MOST FRIGHTENING MOMENT: I have been in four accidents all of which could have ended my life. I nearly drowned at twelve, but was resuscitated. Dad saved me and almost drowned himself. He told me he fought like hell to keep me out of the water. I also witnessed a guy shooting a woman in a church. She had been nursing my brother but had just put him down. It was a .38 calibre shotgun and he just sat there and waited to be arrested. It was very scary.

FIRST KISS: My mother says I was a notorious flirt as a child. I remember having a gigantic crush on this red-headed girl in the first grade who let me buy her candy. She accepted my favours then told me to shove off. But I managed to get one kiss in.

FIRST SEXUAL EXPERIENCE: I was eight when I technically lost my virginity and she was eleven or twelve. She was a girl in the neighbourhood who would take us all round the back of the housing block in Daytona, Florida. We kept our clothes on and moved around. It wasn't disappointing but it did get better with the years! I used condoms and I quite liked them. I am not going to tell you her name.

ELTON JOHN

REAL NAME: Reginald Kenneth Dwight.
BORN: 25/3/1947. Aries. Pinner, Middlesex.
HEIGHT: 5ft 8ins.
NICKNAME: I called myself Elton John after John Baldrey and Elton Dean — two guys in my first band.
SCHOOL: Diford School, Pinner. I was a shy, dumpy kid who wore glasses. But I worked hard.
FIRST JOB: I was a messenger boy for Dick James Music.
INTO THE BIZ: I used to play the piano at the Northwood Hills hotel for £1 a night. I was so nervous of playing alone that my mum always came to watch.
FIRST PERFORMANCE: It was in 1961 with a band called Bluesology.
GREATEST MOMENT: Every day is a very special day because I am healthy.
MOST EMBARRASSING MOMENT: The most embarrassing thing that has ever happened to me was when George Michael and Andrew Ridgeley persuaded me to dress up in a Ronald McDonald costume and join them on stage for Wham!'s farewell concert at Wembley Stadium. As soon as I walked on stage, they both walked off. There I was in front of 70,000 people and everyone of them laughed at me. I stood there for ten minutes before they came back out. I was humiliated!
CARS: My first car was an Austin A40. Now I've got loads of them — I love nice cars. I've got three Aston Martin Vantages, a Rolls Royce Phantom, two Rolls Royce Corniches, four Bentley turbos, a Ferrari Testarossa, a Porche 911 and an E-type Jaguar.
HOME: I'm having a place done up near Windsor — it's going to be great when it is finished and so it should be for the amount of money I am paying!
FOOD: I love Indian — a good curry is a wonderful thing.
MUSIC: I buy three of everything released in all formats, album, CD and tape. My favourites would have to be Dr John, Leon Russell and George Michael.

FILM: I enjoyed playing the Pinball Wizard in *Tommy*. It was very funny because Rod Stewart was originally asked to do it, but I advised him not to. Then I was offered it later, read the script and decided to do it! Rod was not very happy when he found out.

ADMIRES: George Michael — I have watched him mature into a great songwriter. George is a huge talent and a great guy.

HATES: I hate plastic flowers. I have a complete phobia about them. Whenever I go to hotels I have them thrown out and have fresh ones put in.

HOBBIES: I like collecting art. I've got a few Rembrandts and Picassos. I gave one of the Picassos to Rod Stewart for Christmas once and he hung it in his toilet. I love cricket too. I once played a game at Lords with my hair dyed green especially for the occasion.

AMBITION: To carry on doing what I'm doing now.

WILDEST PARTY: I love parties and I've either been to or held some of the best ever. But nothing quite compared to the night I hired the Magic Mountain in Los Angeles and threw a party for Sylvester Stallone. The whole of Hollywood turned up for that one — it was wild.

MOST FRIGHTENING MOMENT: I hate frogs. I remember being about to jump into a pool in Hollywood when I suddenly saw one lying there. I was terrified, but Katharine Hepburn was passing by on her bike and she dived in and fished it out for me.

FIRST SEXUAL EXPERIENCE: I'm not saying.

The piano man. Elton John has always been more outrageous and flamboyant than anyone else

Annie Lennox

REAL NAME: Ann Lennox.

BORN: 25/12/1954. Capricorn. Aberdeen, Scotland.

HEIGHT: 5ft 8ins.

NICKNAME: 'Annie'.

SCHOOL: I got seven O—levels and three A—levels. But I wasn't too bothered. I left to go to the Guildhall to study the flute.

FIRST JOBS: I worked as a waitress, as a salesgirl, in a bookstore, a greengrocer's and even in Mothercare. I was also a fish filleter in a factory. I earned £9.50 for a forty-hour week and the stench made me sick. I sold second-hand clothes in Camden market.

INTO THE BIZ: Dave Stewart walked into a restaurant where I was working and asked me to marry him! We formed the Tourists soon afterwards and that was that.

FIRST PERFORMANCE: When I was about seven at a music festival in Aberdeen. They have an annual festival there for all the schools to participate in. The song I did went, 'My banty hen has laid an egg, I'm having it for tea'. I don't think there'll be any reason for doing it again.

MOST NERVE-WRACKING EXPERIENCE: When the Tourists had to disband because of debts.

GREATEST MOMENT: Getting an American Grammy award for 'Sweet Dreams' and being voted Best British Female Singer in 1984 at the BPI awards.

BIGGEST COCK-UP: Being asked by an American magazine for proof of my sex! It was the *National Enquirer* and they honestly thought I was a man. Needless to say I did not give them the required evidence . . .

CAR: I don't have one.

HOME: I live in Paris with my husband Uli above an old bakery.

HOLIDAYS: Yugoslavia — I like sun, sea and peace.

FOOD: Fresh clean vegetables and fruit. I like Japanese because it's well presented and they take a lot of care over it.

DRINK: Margarita from Ferdinand's in Chalk Farm, London.

MUSIC: Aretha Franklin, Billie Holiday and David Bowie.

FIRST RECORD: 'A Whiter Shade of Pale' by Procol Harum. It was a big hit at the time and I got it especially to take along to a party. My first album was the soundtrack to *Mary Poppins*.

Eurythmics stars Dave Stewart and Annie
Lennox sandwich ex-Beatle George
Harrison after a show in London

FAVE RECORD: David Bowie's 'Let's Dance' — it's fantastic.

HOBBIES: I am taking time off at the moment to help the homeless so that has become my hobby.

FILMS: *Fantasia* and anything with Bob Hope and Bing Crosby.

ADMIRES: Tammy Wynette. I loved her autobiography — she had such a terribly hard life.

AMBITION: To make a few films.

HATES: Bigotry and small-minded people.

FANCIES: David Bowie. And I used to quite fancy Terry Hall of the Fun Boy Three.

MOST FRIGHTENING MOMENT: I got terrible claustrophobia on a plane from the Australian mainland to Tasmania. I was sweating and desperately wanted to get out. I am still terrified of flying.

FIRST KISS: My teddy bear!

FIRST SEXUAL EXPERIENCE: I'm not saying.

SIMON LE BON

FULL NAME: Simon John Le Bon.

BORN: 27/10/1958. Scorpio. Bushey, Hertfordshire.

HEIGHT: 6ft 2ins.

FIRST JOBS: I did loads. I was a photographic printer and developer, warehouseman, hospital porter, tractor driver, tree surgeon, lumberjack and actor!

INTO THE BIZ: I appeared in a Persil TV ad when I was five. I was the kid in the grey and white shirt. My mum used to send me to the studio because we needed the money.

MOST NERVE-WRACKING EXPERIENCE: My first date with Yasmin. We went to the premiere of *Indiana Jones and the Temple of Doom* at Wimbledon, but we were both so nervous we drank half a bottle of Scotch before we got there.

GREATEST MOMENT: When my daughter Amber Rose was born.

BIGGEST COCK-UP: A girl just walked up to me in a nightclub and stuck her hands down the front of my trousers. I couldn't believe it. I said something like: 'Get those out of there.' She was drunk and just stood there grinning. And I remember being embarrassed when a girl in Hungary walked up to me and calmly handed me a condom!

CAR: I drive a £32,000 black Range Rover but the car I have always wanted is an Aston Martin DB6 MkII. I've also got a 30ft yacht worth about £35,000.

HOME: I live in a town house in Chelsea in London.

HOLIDAYS: Montserrat in the Caribbean and the Sahara.

Recognise the guy on the right? Probably not but he has got a famous son — meet Simon Le Bon's parents

Simon Le Bon out on the town with his stunning wife Yasmin, one of the world's highest paid models

FOOD: I'm a vegetarian and my favourite food is angel hair pasta with porcini sauce and I am also partial to honey.

DRINK: You can't beat Krug champagne and I like lagers like Red Stripe and Budweiser.

MUSIC: I like Prince, Joni Mitchell, Jim Morrison, the Cocteau Twins and Patti Smith. But my favourite band of all time would have to be the Rolling Stones.

FIRST RECORD: 'The Lamb Lies Down On Broadway' by Genesis.

FAVE RECORD: 'Love Her Madly' by the Doors.

HOBBIES: Bee-keeping is my favourite hobby at the moment. And I like art, sailing, swimming and water sports. Recently I've taken up a keep fit programme in a big way.

FILM: *Scandal* is the best film I have ever seen.

AMBITION: To learn to fly a helicopter.

HATES: Stepping in dog mess. I loathe that moment when you realise you have done it. I also loathe real ale and bad hotels.

FANCIES: My wife Yasmin, of course.

MOST FRIGHTENING MOMENT: When *Drum,* my boat, sank. It's not often one stares into the ugly black sockets of the big skull, the big D — DEATH. But I couldn't drown — Yasmin would have killed me! I knew that if I breathed in I would die — it was sheer willpower and a desperation to live that kept me alive.

FIRST SEXUAL EXPERIENCE: It was great, in the school playing field. I'm not saying her name because she may be married and her husband would have a fit!

Betty Boo

REAL NAME: Alison Clarkson.

BORN: 6/3/1970. Aries. Kensington, West London.

HEIGHT: 5ft 6ins.

NICKNAME: 'Miss Boo'.

SCHOOL: I deteriorated in the fifth year. I did my O–levels but only got away with two — English and fashion. I started doing A–levels but left before the end. I got terrible reports and the teachers were always telling me I would never get on. The only thing I was good at was sport. I did a lot of rowing, netball and even played five-a-side football for a girls' team in Harrow, North London.

FIRST JOBS: I had a Saturday job in a Dorothy Perkins fashion shop as a sales assistant and they made me work Thursday evenings. I also worked in Marks and Spencer's. I liked it there, but only because the food was good. I also used to work for community transport, Dial-a-Ride.

INTO THE BIZ: I just walked into a record company called Rhythm King one day and played them a demo. I was with a group called Hit and Run. The record boss was really nice to me and had time for me — he gave me my chance.

FIRST PERFORMANCE: I used to be in a group called the She Rockers up until 1988 and my first performance was in 1987 in Wormwood Scrubs, in a place just outside the prison.

MOST NERVE-WRACKING EXPERIENCE: Going for a job as a sound engineer at the BBC after I had done a college course to get into broadcasting. When I was interviewed it was like an exam. He asked me about polar patterns and microphones and I wasn't expecting that at all. I was really nervous about the whole thing. I didn't get the job.

GREATEST MOMENT: I remember feeling really pleased when I scored my first goal in football for Harrow. There were a lot of people there and they really cheered for me.

BIGGEST COCK-UP: I did a radio station interview in London and I swore under my breath. I said 'fuck' and it came out on air. It was really embarrassing because it was live.

CAR: I don't drive but if I did I would like one of those new Mazdas. I like them because they are really dinky and small.

HOMES: First home was a flat in Kensington. Now I have a house in Shepherd's Bush, West London.

HOLIDAYS: I don't take holidays because they are boring. All you do is lie in the sun all day.

FOOD: Chinese. I like chicken with bean sauce.

DRINKS: I usually drink soft drinks like Coke or virgin coladas because they taste like milkshakes! If I drink alcohol I like a lager.

Betty who? Then she was just a forlorn three-year-old but now Betty Boo has hit the big time

Betty Boo looks turtley crazy for movie star Leonardo, but rumours of a romance have been denied

6.2.84 - 29.6.84

SUBJECT	EFFORT GRADE	EXAM MARK	REMARKS
MATHEMATICS	B	39	Alison has tried hard although she still lacks in mathematical confidence. She must learn that to try and then fail does have a place in mathematics.
ENGLISH	B+	64%	Since parents' evening, Alison's attitude has greatly improved, and in particular she has done some very good homework. Her essay work on examination was very well done. Her comprehension paper was middling - more practice is needed, and her mark on the set texts was very low - did she study these? G.B.
FRENCH	A	87%	I am so pleased to see such a dramatic change in Alison's attitude. She is now enthusiastic, co-operative and using her ability fully. She is back to her former self. Well done!
HISTORY	C+	46%	Alison's term work is of a good standard. However, her exam result was very disappointing. She must revise more thoroughly as I am sure it was not lack of ability which let her down.
GEOGRAPHY	B	41%	Alison has taken her work and revision very seriously. Her mark is reasonable - for what was an extremely difficult test. I hope she maintains her progress
ART	B	65%	Alison has maintained her high standard of work and continues to make progress. I hope she will keep this effort up in the fourth year.
DRAMA			
MUSIC	B+	65%	Alison has worked well this year and I am very pleased with her progress. R. Fita.
PHYSICAL EDUCATION	A		A delight to teach. Alison has worked hard this year, and has made excellent progress at rowing. I hope she will carry on the good work.
RELIGIOUS EDUCATION	C	26	Alison is a quiet worker but the lack of enthusiasm was reflected in a poor examination result. She has made progress
TEXTILES	A-	55	Alison is a acceptable pupil, she has achieved an excellent standard in Textiles.
HOME ECONOMICS	C	41½%	A deterioration in Alison's attitude to this subject has been noted this half-year. A pity, as she is capable of better results.
SCIENCE	B-	61	Alison has worked well for most of this year. I hope she will not allow herself to be distracted from her work next year.
			Spence. Acting Deputy Head

EFFORT GRADES FOR GROUP
A: EXCELLENT   B: ABOVE AVERAGE   C: AVERAGE   D: BELOW AVERAGE   E: POOR

Hammersmith School was pleased with
the fourteen-year-old Alison's progress.
Now they must be even more pleased
with 'old girl' Betty Boo's success

MUSIC: I like pop and classical music. Lisa Stansfield is my favourite singer.
FIRST RECORD: 'Pop Music' by M.
FAVE RECORD: Salt 'N' Pepa's first album.
FILM: I liked *The Untouchables*. Sean Connery used to be my grandmother's milk boy in Edinburgh!
ADMIRES: Phil Collins and Madonna — she is so determined and extra fit.
AMBITION: I wanted to become a policeman — now I just want to be more successful.
HATES: I hate cruelty to animals.
FANCIES: Richard Gere, he is gorgeous.
MOST FRIGHTENING MOMENT: I had two car crashes last year and hurt my neck. And I don't like flying because you are not in control. I find take-offs just awful. I always imagine the plane will explode.
WILDEST PARTY: Christmas last year was wild because I went out every single night and got drunk. The drinks were free. It was great.
FIRST KISS: It was horrible because I had to wear a brace and he didn't know about it. I was fifteen and at school. He was the school heart-throb and everyone hated me because they were all jealous. His name was Francisco Ferraro.
FIRST SEXUAL EXPERIENCE: It was neither good nor bad. All my mates had done it and so I thought I'd have a go. I was seventeen at the time. It was at his house. We couldn't do it at my house because my mum and dad were there. It was just very quiet. His name was John.

DAVID BOWIE

REAL NAME: David Robert Jones.
BORN: 8/1/1947. Capricorn. Brixton, South London.
HEIGHT: 5ft 10ins.
NICKNAME: I don't have one.
SCHOOL: I was thrown out of the Stansfield Road Junior School choir for making too much noise — I was always singing and joking.
FIRST JOB: I was a commercial artist for six months after leaving art school. I had no interest in it at all. It was boring so I quit.

Queen stars Roger Taylor and Brian May
fill David Bowie in on the latest gossip at
Live Aid

INTO THE BIZ: I was a saxophone player in a band called the Konrads, who hung around in Bromley. I wasn't allowed to sing at first — they didn't rate me!

FIRST PERFORMANCE: At Bromley Technical High School. I was incredibly nervous but it went OK.

MOST NERVE-WRACKING EXPERIENCE: On a plane on the Glass Spider tour. The plane was called back as it was about to take off from Rome airport and everybody thought there was a bomb on board. It was only when we came to a halt that we discovered the real reason — the chief of police wanted my autograph! I was not so much annoyed as stunned — that could only happen in Italy!

GREATEST MOMENT: In Barcelona on 16 September 1990. That was the last time I played my best known songs in Europe. It was very emotional for me and the crowd knew that — they brought me back for *seven* encores. It was a fitting place to put Ziggy Stardust to rest.

BIGGEST COCK-UP: Taking drugs. I went through hell when I was younger, mainly on cocaine and it was a total waste of time.

CAR: I have just the one — a ten-year-old Volvo in Switzerland. I am not really into cars.

C'est la Viz. David Bowie catches up on the latest saucy nonsense from Britain's fastest growing mag, *Viz*

HOMES: My first home was in Brixton, South London. Now I have three — one in Lausanne, Switzerland, one in Mustique and one in Australia.

HOLIDAYS: Indonesia and Australia. I try to get to Bali once a year — it's a stunningly beautiful place.

FOOD: I am very keen on Japanese, Indonesian and Italian. My favourite restaurant is Sabatini in Rome.

DRINK: I love a very strong Italian coffee which I have flown in to wherever I am in the world.

MUSIC: My favourite bands at the moment would be the Pixies and Sonic Youth. But I will always love the Stones, the Beatles and Elvis.

FIRST RECORD: Little Richard with 'Lonely Girl'.

FAVE RECORD: Almost impossible but 'Wild is the Wind' by Nina Simone would have to be my choice.

FILMS: *Brief Encounter* for its Englishness and *Mean Streets* for its Americanness.

HOBBIES: Art, painting and visiting museums. I reckon I've seen every major painting in the western world. I go to art galleries in every town or city I play in. And I paint a lot. I've got a self-portrait and one I did of Iggy Pop on my walls. I also love reading. On the last tour I had a special trunk for all my books. I can get through one a day when I'm going well.

ADMIRES: Montgomery Clift, Martin Scorcese.

AMBITION: To be very busy. I want to carry on being incredibly busy. I have a very inquisitive mind. I want to learn.

HATES: Ignorance.

BEST FRIEND: Coco Schwab.

FANCIES: In every city I drive past a stunningly beautiful girl and I never get to say hello.

MOST FRIGHTENING MOMENT: It was during the filming of *Merry Christmas Mr Lawrence.* I was buried up to my neck in sand on this beach in the South Sea Islands. They dug a hole underneath my body so there was plenty of air about but that also attracted rats — all I could feel was these rodents biting at my feet. It was terrifying. And I remember driving in the outback in Australia, with my band Tin Machine when a huge spider landed on my steering wheel. I swerved all over the place out of sheer fright. I never did find out what it was but there are some lethal ones out there.

WILDEST PARTY: The Serious Moonlight tour was a virtual non-stop party especially when the Duran Duran boys turned up in Sydney — they were pretty wild guys then.

FIRST KISS: I can't remember who she was but I was about seven years old. It was pretty momentous as I recall!

FIRST SEXUAL EXPERIENCE: It was unforgettable if only because I had to clamber out of the girl's first-floor bedroom window to avoid her parents. I would have been about fifteen, I think. I got away with it though.

M C Hammer

REAL NAME: Stanley Kirk Burrell.

BORN: Oakland, California.

HEIGHT: 5ft 10ins.

NICKNAME: I got the name 'Hammer' because a mate of mine thought I looked exactly like a baseball star called Hank 'Hammer' Aaron. The 'M C' stands for master of ceremonies.

SCHOOL: I wasn't really into school. I left as soon as I could to join the US navy. I was stationed in California for most of the three years, though I did spend six months in Japan.

INTO THE BIZ: I discharged myself from the navy and formed a religious rap band called the Holy Ghost Boys. Then I decided to make a rap record. I put a lot of money I saved into it and it ended up selling 50,000 copies — all made from the basement of my house.

MOST NERVE-WRACKING EXPERIENCE: I had a try out for the San Francisco Giants baseball team but got rejected. It was a terrible moment. I had always dreamed of being a baseball star since the age of eight when I was hired as an errand boy for the local Oaklands team — I carried the bats.

GREATEST MOMENT: When I heard that my album had become the biggest selling rap album of all time. I had made a bet with Capitol Records that it would break the record and they promised me a £150,000 Ferrari Testarossa if it did. Now they've bought me a beauty — it does 0-60 in 3.3 seconds. Winning the MTV awards for best artist and best video was another great moment.

BIGGEST COCK-UP: If you look closely at the video for 'Have You Seen Her?', you can see my bum. At the time I wanted to do it, and all the girls say they love that bit. But I find it really embarrassing to look at now.

CARS: I own seven cars — a Porsche, three Mercedes, a Corvette, and two others. The Porsche is my favourite — it can do 0-60 in 3.9 seconds. It makes me stain my pants!

It's Hammer time. Rap superstar MC Hammer has every reason to grin. His first album sold more than 7 million copies

HOME: I live in a huge house in Oakland, California with my wife and two-year-old daughter.

MUSIC: Bobby Brown told me he thought I was one of the world's greatest dancers. I told him I think he is too! I'm also really into the Teenage Mutant Ninja Turtles. I recorded one of the tracks for their movie. I used to model myself on James Brown — he was amazing.

HOBBIES: Poetry.

ADMIRES: Bobby Brown — he is a great friend of mine.

AMBITION: I always wanted to be a TV sports reporter. And I would love to make a movie. I work very hard — I sometimes go three whole days without any sleep.

HATES: Violence, drugs, swearing and gold chains.

MOST FRIGHTENING MOMENT: Every time I set foot in my Porsche. It scares the hell out of me.

MICK JAGGER

FULL NAME: Michael Phillip Jagger.

BORN: 26/7/1943. Leo. Dartford, Kent.

HEIGHT: 5ft 7ins.

NICKNAME: 'Rubber-lips' seems to be what most people call me.

SCHOOL: I went to the London School of Economics in 1960. I was really hip with the tightest drainpipes and longest hair. I was rebellious and studious — working hard because my dad told me to. At school, I remember skiving off the cross-country runs and going to the sand dunes to talk about girls.

FIRST JOB: I earned £5 for appearing on a children's TV show called 'Watching Sport' where I demonstrated my skill with a kayak.

INTO THE BIZ: I bumped into Keith Richards on a train and we started working together in London and formed a band called Little Boy Blue and the Blue Boys.

FIRST PERFORMANCE: We were booked to appear on BBC Radio's 'Jazz Club', but the contract said we could only have six players — so I had to stand down because I was only a singer. The first show was at the Ealing Jazz Club in 1963, I remember our first TV show a year later because the producer said afterwards that we would never get anywhere with that 'vile-looking singer with tyre-tread lips.'

MOST NERVE-WRACKING EXPERIENCE: On stage at Altamount in Oregon with the Hell's Angels. I still get a lot of death threats from Angels.

GREATEST MOMENT: The day I bought a pink Cadillac in Los Angeles — it was something I had always dreamed about and it did not let me down. It was a fantastic moment driving it away and knowing it was all mine!

BIGGEST COCK-UP: When me, Billy Wyman and Brian Jones were fined £5 for insulting behaviour after we passed water against a garage wall in West Ham in London. It was embarrassing appearing in court about it, I suppose.

CARS: I recently bought a very expensive Ferrari. My first car was a Ford, I think. I remember being fined £16 for driving it without insurance and breaking the speed limit in 1964.

HOMES: I have four — in Mustique, New York, London and France.

HOLIDAYS: Barbados for the cricket.

FOOD: I eat anything healthy. My favourite restaurant would be San Lorenzo, an Italian restaurant in Knightsbridge, London. I also like cooking, especially Vietnamese food. My favourite dish is apple pie, I love the pastry crust.

DRINKS: White wine and champagne. I always give it up for the forty days of Lent.

MUSIC: I like Prince, Muddy Waters, the Police when they were on stage and Elvis Costello on record.

FIRST RECORD: Muddy Waters *Live at Newport* — I still listen to it.

FAVE RECORD: It changes daily.

HOBBIES: Cricket, antiques and keeping fit. I run seven miles a day when I am on tour.

FILM: I like a lot of films but nothing I have appeared in. I made some dumb movies.

ADMIRES: I admire Margaret Thatcher. The Tories are always trying to get me to support them officially but I don't want to get into that game.

AMBITION: To make a good movie.

HATES: I despise the cliché-ridden sentimentality that people like Frank Sinatra produce. It's just awful. I've also got no time for drugs any more. I tried them all and wouldn't recommend any of them.

FANCIES: Jerry.

MOST FRIGHTENING MOMENT: I pulled a gun on Keith Moon from the Who when I thought he was a burglar trying to break into my honeymoon suite in a New

The world's most glamorous showbiz couple, Mick Jagger and Jerry Hall off to another star-studded party. It's tough being a rolling stone

York hotel after my marriage to Bianca. He climbed through the window for a laugh — but I didn't know it was him. He thought it was all very funny.

WILDEST PARTY: The reception party for the *Beggars' Banquet* album in London. It ended with a massive custard pie fight — very silly but good fun.

FIRST SEXUAL EXPERIENCE: I was twelve and it was with two schoolgirls in a garden shed. That's all I am telling you.

Michael McDonald

FULL NAME: Michael Hanley McDonald.

BORN: 12/2/1952. Aquarius. St. Louis, Missouri.

HEIGHT: 5ft 11ins.

NICKNAME: 'The Mole' — that is what one of my old mates used to call me at high school but I have no idea why!

SCHOOL: It started out OK but I left when I was sixteen or seventeen without doing the exams. I did go back to school years later to take them because it was always at the back of mind that I might need them if the music failed.

FIRST JOBS: I did a paper round when I was nine or ten but it was fairly unsuccessful and I was fired the next day! I was also a stockroom boy at the local store, unloading trucks and things.

INTO THE BIZ: I was always mucking around with instruments when I was young — it was almost inevitable that I would go into the business. I never really thought about anything else.

FIRST PERFORMANCE: I played at a church dance and made £4. My sister Kathy was in charge. I was about twelve at the time.

MOST NERVE-WRACKING EXPERIENCE: When I played with the Doobie Brothers, there was one bit where we had to leap into the audience. Unfortunately, one night all the fans grabbed my guitar and tore it to pieces. Perhaps they didn't like the music?

GREATEST MOMENT: Supporting Tina Turner at Woburn Abbey — it was a fantastic night.

BIGGEST COCK-UP: One night during a gig in Detroit I got hit in the face with a tennis shoe. It stung like hell and it was also a bit humiliating continuing the show with tennis shoe tread on my face.

CARS: My first car was a 1957 Dodge station wagon. Now I drive a Chevvy truck and my wife drives a Mercedes.

HOMES: My first was in St. Louis, now I live in a three-bedroom cottage in Santa Barbara, California. I love it there.

HOLIDAYS: I love going to Europe and I often go to Hawaii.

FOOD: Mexican.

DRINK: I don't touch alcohol now. I used to be an alcoholic but I gave it up in 1986. Now I drink water.

Michael McDonald supported Tina Turner on her recent tour and that propelled him into superstardom(*Photo: Brian Aris*)

MUSIC: I do tend to be a good ten years behind everyone else. I listen to oldies and that is where I get my inspiration for my writing. I do like a lot of contemporary music, but more often than not I prefer something older. Ray Charles is my all-time favourite.

FIRST RECORD: 'Wake Up Little Susie' by the Everley Brothers.

FAVE RECORD: Marvin Gaye's *SuperHits*.

HOBBIES: Surfing.

FILM: I loved *Batman*. Jack Nicholson's a brilliant actor.

ADMIRES: Ray Charles and my wife.

AMBITION: Apart from playing music I would like to think I could get into parenthood.

HATES: Drugs. I got involved with cocaine when I was with the Doobie Brothers and it almost ruined my life. But I got out and I've been clean for years now.

FANCIES: I can't tell you — my wife would kill me!

FIRST KISS: It was terrible but I do remember it pretty vividly. I was about twelve. The girl I kissed smoked a lot and a friend of mine set the whole thing up. The one thing I remember most about her was her weird haircut. I think her name was Sandy.

FIRST SEXUAL EXPERIENCE: It was pretty bad. I was about fourteen or fifteen at the time. It was a very traumatic experience — I think there are a lot of complexities with that sort of relationship at that age.

STARRY COMPANY FOR THE AUTHORS